# THE 1913 McKINNEY STORE COLLAPSE

CAROL O'KEEFE WILSON

THE History PRESS

Published by The History Press
Charleston, SC
www.historypress.com

Copyright © 2018 by Carol Wilson
All rights reserved

*Front cover*: The scene of the accident. *Courtesy of Bob Patterson of Lafayette, Louisiana.*
*Opposite: Courtesy of Robert W. Scott.*

First published 2018

Manufactured in the United States

ISBN 9781467139502

Library of Congress Control Number: 2018936069

*Notice*: The information in this book is true and complete to the best of our knowledge. It is offered without guarantee on the part of the author or The History Press. The author and The History Press disclaim all liability in connection with the use of this book.

All rights reserved. No part of this book may be reproduced or transmitted in any form whatsoever without prior written permission from the publisher except in the case of brief quotations embodied in critical articles and reviews.

*This book is dedicated to the memory of Robert Norman Presley.*

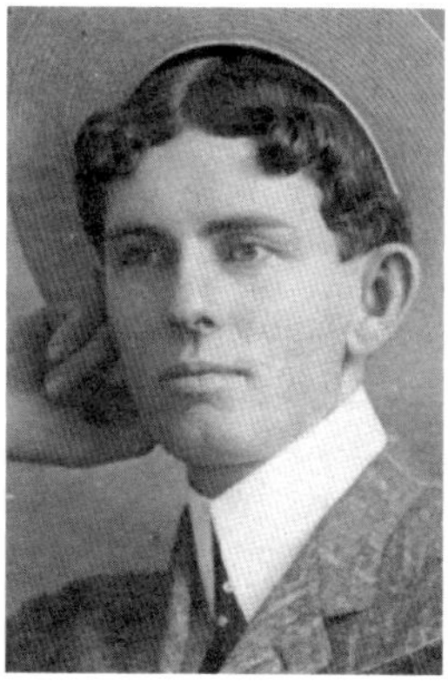

# CONTENTS

# PREFACE

This book is heavily imprinted with the work of a man named Walter Buckner Wilson (1869–1946), a McKinney newspaper owner/editor and local historian. Wilson, a man who had his finger on the pulse of activity in Collin County for more than half a century, deserves credit for chronicling local history that extended well beyond his duty as a newsman. In his role as journalist, he captured the details of many events over the years, but Wilson recorded *this* story—the deadly collapse of two buildings on McKinney's town square in 1913—from firsthand knowledge. Because he was working in his nearby office when the two downtown stores suddenly sank into a pile of debris, Wilson was among the first on the scene. He spent more than eight hours working the accident, first as a rescuer and later in his role as journalist, summoning a photographer to capture the scene and wiring details of the catastrophe to affiliate newspapers. But apart from Wilson's intimate knowledge about this incident, he had another unique link to the subject matter. He was vocal about such risks.

On January 23, 1913, Wilson and his partner Tom W. Perkins released their weekly newspaper, the *Weekly Democrat-Gazette*, as usual. At that time, Wilson could not have imagined that January 23 would register as one of the most significant days in McKinney's history, nor could he have imagined that his newspaper carried an eerie forewarning about the day's events.

Buried on page 8, the morning's *Gazette* carried a plea for public action regarding the Central Ward Elementary School, because the old building suffered from serious structural issues. At the bequest of school board members, a slew of building inspectors had taken turns examining the building, but none had offered the firm condemnation board members needed to garner public support for financing a new school. According to the *Gazette*, one of those structural experts offered this particularly poor advice: "He assures the board that an old building, especially one as old as this one, would give ample warning in case it threatened to collapse."[1]

By the purest coincidence, only a few hours after the *Gazette*'s appeal for a new school was released as part of the day's news, the citizens of McKinney learned firsthand that an unstable building offers no notice when it succumbs to the pressure of excessive weight, time and wear. It was not the aging schoolhouse that dispensed that dreadful lesson; rather, it was two stores that took a deadly tumble that afternoon, spilling mortar, glass, bricks, merchandise and blood on the northeast corner of the town square.

Walter Wilson, who was trying to raise public awareness about such danger, deserves credit for saving lives that day. Whether or not he gave any thought to the acute irony of the day, we do not know.

The following week's issues of the *McKinney Democrat-Gazette* and its rival, the weekly *McKinney Examiner*, were laden with bold and heartrending headlines that dominated most pages. But one tragedy may have prevented another. Among the features was an announcement that all 256 students attending the Central Ward School were being reassigned to other schools, effective immediately.

In addition to the work Walter Wilson did every day as a journalist, he made considerable contributions to the recorded history of Collin County during his life, interviewing early residents, archiving articles from other newspapers into bulging scrapbooks and maintaining a personal journal. I drew heavily from his work, particularly his newspapers. In the few instances where there was conflicting information, I gave preference to Wilson's views and wisdom.

Although I would be proud to claim a kinship with Walter Wilson, we are not related.

# ACKNOWLEDGEMENTS

This book is unique in terms of its sourcing, a fact that presented a special challenge to this writer. A glance at the bibliography highlights the fact that few books contain any reference to this topic. In researching the story, I relied heavily on three sources: period newspapers, court records pertaining to a trial that resulted from the accident and information and photos supplied by descendants of people involved in the tragedy. Because the body of useful resources was so limited, and because it is often difficult to locate descendants, every contact was critically important to me.

I do not live in McKinney and had no knowledge of the area's history when I began this project, making it imperative that I establish a local contact in that city early on. Luckily, I found the Collin County History Museum and, more specifically, curator Deborah Kilgore, to guide me. Deborah's help was invaluable, including an impromptu walking tour she provided of the McKinney Square. Dirk Hedges of the McKinney Fire Department was gracious in allowing me to make an unscheduled visit to the department's museum. Both of the aforementioned museums are well worth a visit. Guy Giersch, McKinney's historic preservation officer, was also most helpful, as was local historian Joy Gough.

I cannot overstate the value of the archive of McKinney newspapers that was available to me through The Portal to Texas History, a service provided by the University of North Texas. I simply could not have written this story without easy access to those expertly archived newspapers.

Thank you Crystal Brooks and Priscilla Escobedo, associates with the Dallas History & Archives Division of the Dallas Library system. Priscilla was patient and helpful through many e-mail inquiries. I would also like to thank the staff at the Briscoe Center for American History in Austin for accommodating my requests and pulling many spools of microfilm from off-site storage.

Other enthusiasts of local history were helpful in supplying leads and information. In this category, I wish to thank Marianne Wells, Kenny Bush, John Brooks and Bob Patterson. Bob furnished the cover photo when I had almost given up hope of finding it. Thank you, Nancy Shepperd of Photo Concepts, for expertly improving the quality of some of the old newspaper photos.

As part of my research, I was fortunate to meet, via e-mail and phone, several descendants of family members of characters in this story. Specifically, I would like to mention these people:

Robert Scott, son of Emma Lou Presley Scott and grandson of Norman and Sophia Presley

John Mack Thomas, grandson of John W. and Stella Thomas and great-grandson of Elder R.C. Horn

Martha Prince, granddaughter of Lelia and Robert Hight (daughter of Eugene Hight)

Barbara Ware, granddaughter of Lelia and Robert Hight (daughter of Kathryn Hight)

Ferol Richardson, great-granddaughter of Patrick Cheeves

Ed Hinkle, widower of Patsy Hinkle, who was the granddaughter of Patrick Cheeves

Bess Miller, the youngest child of Luther Stephenson

David Miller, a distant relative of Ike Talkington

Nan Shirley, wife of a grandson of Mort and Iva Shirley

Robert Shirley, son of Jack Shirley, grandson of Mort and Iva Shirley

Amoret Cain, great-granddaughter of Elder R.C. Horn

Clyde Geer, great-grandson of Elder R.C. Horn

Kevin McCulloch, cousin to the Cheeves brothers

Nancy Bush Morian, granddaughter of Leslie Walker Bush

To those who supplied images, I offer an additional salute. In most cases, you were *the only person* who could have provided this unique and meaningful addition. In particular, I want to say that I enjoyed corresponding with John Mack Thomas and his wife, Ann, and appreciate their help and their interest in the project. Lastly, I wish to thank The History Press for preserving this valuable story for the archives of Texas history.

# 1
# OUT OF THE ASHES

In a manner of speaking, the two buildings that collapsed on the public square in McKinney, Texas, on the afternoon of January 23, 1913, were born of misfortune, both having been raised—at least figuratively—out of the ashes of an earlier catastrophe.

The tribulation can be traced specifically to 3:00 a.m., Sunday, June 27, 1875, when the sound of pistol shots signaled residents that a fire was raging in the commercial center of McKinney. The alarm sent most men within earshot scrambling from their beds and into the streets, where they soon realized that the calamity would be one for the record books. The north side of the public square was ablaze, the fire fueled by an overabundance of wooden structures that comprised one side of the outer boundary of the town square. Joined one to another, the buildings were easy prey for the flames. When the blaze reached the end of the row of businesses—to a street that might otherwise have served as a natural barrier—a relentless wind sent live embers in search of new fuel on opposite corners. The fire threatened to annihilate decades of progress and prosperity by destroying the town's largest concentration of assets.[2]

Chief among residents' fears was the loss of the town's imposing new courthouse, then under construction.[3] Work on the building had suffered serious delays—but with good reason. In September 1874, construction had come to an abrupt halt when the brick that was meant to cover the exterior was found to be of poor quality. Locals, who insisted that the new courthouse should reflect high standards, demanded that stone be substituted, even

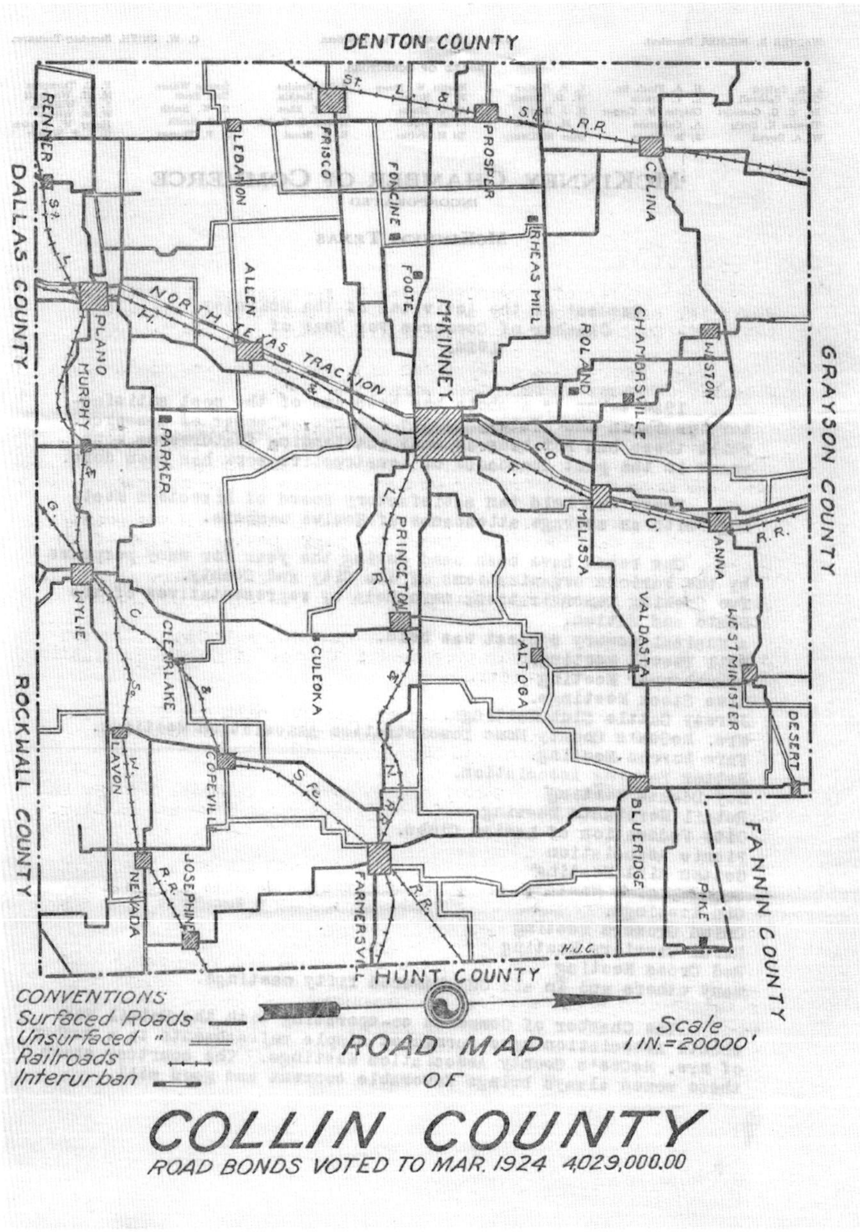


Map of Collin County, circa 1924. *Courtesy of the Briscoe Center for American History, University of Texas at Austin.*

though the switch added $23,500 to the contracted price.[4] In the end, the delay and inconvenience proved worth the effort, but in mid-1875, when the courthouse should have already been in use, it was still several months short of completion.

McKinney, Texas, designated the county seat for Collin County in 1848, was built in a style common to towns that served as county seats in developing southern towns. Early, modest versions of the county courthouse helped center McKinney, but the grand, new and modern courthouse was poised to permanently anchor the space, serving as a nucleus to a public square that facilitated early trading. Neat rows of business houses sprang up around the four sides, and a grid comprising dirt roads radiated out from that hub. The first stores and saloons were constructed of wood, but because fires were so common in those early days—in McKinney and elsewhere—there was a collective plan by property owners to replace burned-out structures with brick when possible. In doing so, property owners were following the lead of an enterprising, German-born man named Abraham Rhine, who built the first brick structure about 1868. Rhine, who also owned a general store in Dallas, sold goods and bartered with men who brought in commodities that were in high demand like furs, pelts and wool. He procured the bricks used to build his McKinney store from a location about twenty miles north of town.[5]

The money that filtered through McKinney's various business houses, to the tune of about $650,000 per year in the late 1870s, was generated almost entirely by products and services related to agriculture.[6] In later days, and for many decades, cotton was a particularly hot commodity, the area's dark, waxy soil being ideal for its growth. But corn, wheat and oats were produced in abundance, as were large quantities and varieties of fruits and vegetables. McKinney-area farmers claimed they had grown beets as long as fifteen inches and weighing more than two pounds and apples with circumferences greater than eleven inches.[7] During a two-month period in the fall of 1875, the year of the great fire, McKinney shipped out 70,000 bushels of wheat, 650,000 bushels of oats, 800,000 pounds of flour and 400 bales of cotton.[8] Cotton later overtook the others as the most heavily traded commodity.

The ability to broker products—often done on the court square, as it was called in those days—was crucial to the flow of commerce, but so was the ability to transport those commodities.[9] When it came to commercial transportation, McKinney was thrice blessed over the years. In 1872, the Houston and Texas Central Railway reached McKinney, sandwiching the

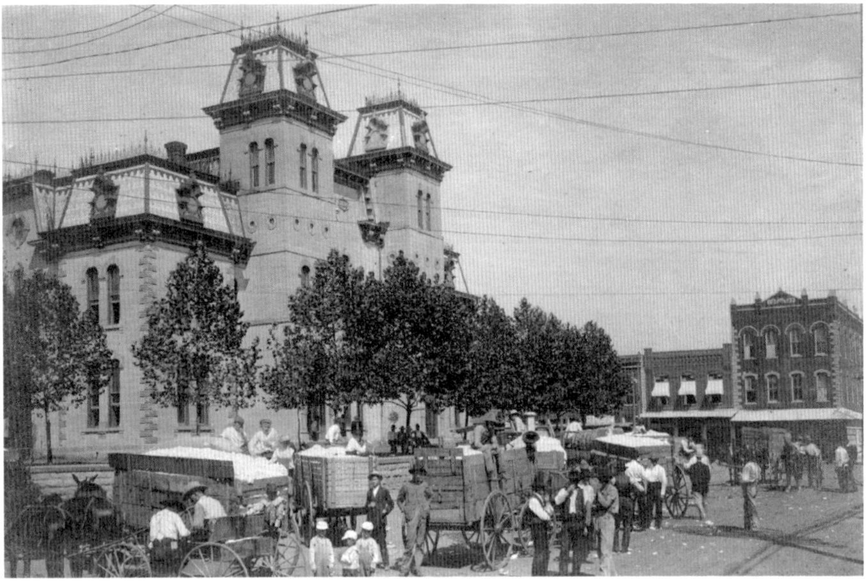

Early shot of the square showing the courthouse and cotton brokering. The two buildings on the right are those that later collapsed. *Courtesy of McKinney Historic Preservation Office.*

town by almost equal distance between Dallas and Sherman. The impact was significant, including the railroad's purchase of eight acres of land near the square, where it constructed a modern depot. But McKinney owed a debt to the railroad that predated the depot and the trains that serviced it. High-paying rail-building jobs offered to locals by the railroad and large numbers of men brought into the area to build the lines launched a decided boom in McKinney in 1871.[10]

The presence of the first rail had a mushrooming effect, incentivizing farmers to produce more, thus stimulating trade that attracted a second line, the Missouri, Kansas and Texas Railroad, in 1881. Finally, in 1908, interurban service linked McKinney to points such as Dallas, Denison and Waco. The interurban was a trolley-like service that transported passengers, stopping at frequent intervals, bringing in businessmen, shoppers and visitors and allowing McKinney residents to travel to nearby cities with ease. The value of these early rail services can hardly be overstated. Many emerging towns watched helplessly as their economies stalled and their populations dwindled after they were excluded from railroad routes.

McKinney's early leaders honored certain southern states, from which many of them had come, when naming the streets that surround the courthouse, a theme that was unique to the public square. Kentucky and Tennessee Streets ran north to south, with Virginia and Louisiana running perpendicular. Each block surrounding the square contained about eight, mostly two-story, commercial buildings. Upper floors were often leased to doctors and attorneys or used as office space or living quarters. Business houses, as they were called, came and went with some frequency, but at any given time, the town square could claim enterprises numbering in the dozens. In the earliest years, the most plentiful businesses were saddle shops, blacksmiths, saloons and dry goods establishments. Later additions included hotels, tinsmiths, cafés, drugstores, grocers and shoemakers. As the town continued to prosper, banks, jewelers, barbers and confectioneries became common. As time passed, the town even had a few innovative female proprietors, such as Willie Emme Marshall, who operated a millinery shop.

McKinney was proud of its prosperity and growth and proud to be the home of James Throckmorton, the twelfth governor of Texas. Throckmorton, who had studied both medicine and law, was an anti-secessionist like Sam Houston, but he was able to put his personal feelings aside and follow the will of the people after Texas seceded. He organized a company of men in Collin County and vigorously fought for the Confederacy until his health failed him. After the war, he ran for governor, hoping to guide the state through the contentious period of Reconstruction, and was handily elected. But Texas did not fare well under military command, and bitter feelings against Throckmorton grew with General Charles Griffith and General Philip Sheridan, who saw him as an obstruction to their notion of progress. The festering relations doomed Throckmorton's chance to hold the office for more than a year. By 1875, James Throckmorton had returned to the public service arena and was serving as a congressman for the state's Third District. Collin County was ever loyal in supporting Throckmorton in his endeavors.

In the predawn hours of 1875, residents of McKinney were determined to hold on to the gains they had made. The fire created a panic that spurred most available men into action—McKinney had no organized fire department so every able-bodied man was drafted into service when the signal came. The men formed bucket brigades, soaking blankets and using them to beat and suffocate the flames. Saturated blankets were also thrown across rooftops of buildings downwind to impede the spread, while storeowners pulled inventory out of their stores in attempts to save it. The heat and smoke were insufferable, causing workers to retreat often. It took the men two full hours of exhaustive work to fully extinguish the flames.

Dawn revealed the charred remains of a dozen businesses and two homes; the heaviest toll was on the north side of the square, where little remained beyond a few blackened stone chimneys. Several other businesses were fortunate to have their losses confined to smoke and water damage. The first men on the scene confirmed the obvious, that the fire had originated on the east end of the north block. The corner building on that east end belonged to the local chapter of the Odd Fellows fraternal order, also known as Empire No. 68. The lodge's commercial neighbor to the immediate west was a saloon and billiards hall known to locals as the Parlor Saloon. These two structures were among the first to perish in the fire, and their replacements would one day be marked as the most infamous buildings in McKinney's history.

The men who fought the fire later mapped out its destructive trajectory. When discovered, the flames had already taken a marked toll on a boardinghouse run by a Mrs. Hurt and on the back portion of the Parlor Saloon. The Odd Fellows hall, located on the upper floor of the building that adjoined the saloon, was the next to go. Lodge members made a frantic and successful attempt to save their records, but nothing else was spared. Every asset belonging to Portwood & Shaw, a dry goods establishment located in the lower level of the lodge building, was consumed. The flames soon took the Murray & McKinney dry goods store, the J.B. Howell drugstore, Winninghoff's Barber Shop, the Dowell House hotel and Walker's Confectionary. On the immediate west side of the Parlor Saloon, the book and stationery store of Seay and Seay soon fell, as did the dry goods store of Estes & Barry. Sam Anderson and T.C. McKinney lost their dwellings.

A young Irishman named Peter Turbitt owned the property where the Parlor Saloon had stood just hours earlier. Turbitt lost his building to the fire, along with its contents, a bar and billiards establishment he owned in partnership with a man named James Ware. Turbitt, who was twenty-eight in 1875, came to the United States from Ireland as a young man and moved to McKinney in 1873.[11] Peter Turbitt placed his loss at $6,000, for which he was entirely uninsured. After the fire, Turbitt and his commercial neighbor, Odd Fellows Empire No. 68, as well as a passel of other businessmen, found themselves unified in their desire to overcome their collective setback. They planned to subscribe to the new conventional wisdom: rebuilding with brick and mortar.

By early the following year, 1876, both Turbitt and lodge leaders were anxious to rebuild the northeast corner of the square. After studying the layout of his property, Turbitt decided he needed to acquire a three-foot, six-inch section of the lodge's property to achieve the architectural footprint he envisioned for his new building. The two parties soon stuck a deal. In exchange for conveyance of the extra footage Turbitt wanted, Turbitt agreed to construct a dividing wall—known as a demising wall—that would be shared by both new structures, with Turbitt supplying both labor and materials. Representatives for the lodge, R.C. White and Isaac Crouch, signed the deed of transfer on February 2, 1876, and Turbitt began construction of the partition wall the following day. The wall was seventeen inches thick, its value placed at $350. With the construction of the dividing wall underway, contractors for the lodge began working on the other three walls of their new building, and Peter Turbitt did likewise.[12]

With their shared wall as a starting point, the two structures quickly took shape, becoming something like Siamese twins joined at the hip. The buildings were raised together in a spirit of great optimism in 1876. Unfortunately, they were destined to go down together thirty-six years later in a display of sheer horror.

# 2
# THOSE ODD FELLOWS

Although the Odd Fellows property and old saloon building shared a major setback in 1875 and later shared a structural wall, the owners of the properties and the histories of the buildings were unique in almost every other sense. The McKinney chapter of the lodge primarily developed the property for its own use; leasing out a portion of the space to earn income was a secondary goal.

The greater Odd Fellows organization can trace its roots back to eighteenth-century England, where, in the absence of social aid programs, the needs of the poor, sick, orphaned and elderly often went unattended. When a group came together and organized with a goal of addressing those needs, the members were initially labeled "odd," which led them to eventually assume the name. The organization still promotes friendship, love and truth and is still known for its charitable work, which favors marginalized elements of society. Chief among the good works of the Odd Fellows in Texas during the early days was the building and support of a large orphans' home established in Corsicana in 1886. Over time, the facility grew into a large complex and expanded its services to include widows and elderly people in need.

McKinney's local Empire No. 68 was organized in 1854 and grew to be one of the state's most significant chapters. In 1870, the local order purchased the lot on the northeast corner of McKinney's square, where it erected a two-story frame building, using the upper floor as a meeting hall and the lower level as a means of earning rental income. The lodge and other property owners on the square understood the value of their location and fought hard to maintain that benefit in 1874 when the plan for a new courthouse included a proposal to relocate the structure. Some leaders floated the idea of building the new courthouse at a distant location to include a park of several acres, but pressure from property owners on the square quickly squelched the plan.[13]

The fire of 1875 temporarily interrupted the group's progress and good fortune. Representatives for the lodge, who placed the value of their five-year-old wooden structure at $3,500, were not listed among the few who had insurance coverage. The tenant on the lower floor, the dry goods establishment of Portwood & Shaw, sustained a loss of inventory, with an estimated valued of $10,000, for which the owners had $6,000 worth of insurance.[14] Lodge members were determined to rebuild using materials less flammable than wood; they did not, however, plan to spring for the extra cost of stone over brick.

As Peter Turbitt began work on the common wall in 1876, lodge representatives chose a pair of Dallas-based contactors named Snowden M. Leftwich and Paul H. Jamison to construct their new building. The partners were best known for erecting the landmark Gaston Building in downtown Dallas, with Leftwich supplying the brick from a large manufacturing plant he owned and Jamison acting as overseer.[15] In later years, members of the lodge reflected on the construction work, saying it had been done under the "advice, direction and supervision" of an architect, but they failed to name the man. Resting on a foundation of rock, the exterior walls, which began at about ground level, were constructed of brick, mortar and stone, with an unnamed number of iron columns set into the front wall for support. The new two-story structure extended back eighty feet, a full ten feet farther than Turbitt's building next door, which was also under construction.[16]

The new building served the needs of the lodge for five years before growth in membership rendered the facility too small. According to legal documents prepared by the lodge many years later, in late May 1891, members laid out a plan to enlarge the building that included extending the length of the structure by 40 feet and adding a third level. The addition of the third floor in 1891 was verified using newspapers, but the Sanborn map pictured here, dated April 1885, seems to show that the Odd Fellows building had already been expanded to 120 feet by that date. There was a large open space behind the saloon building next door to the Odd Fellows building because the Odd Fellows building was almost twice as long as the saloon in 1885.

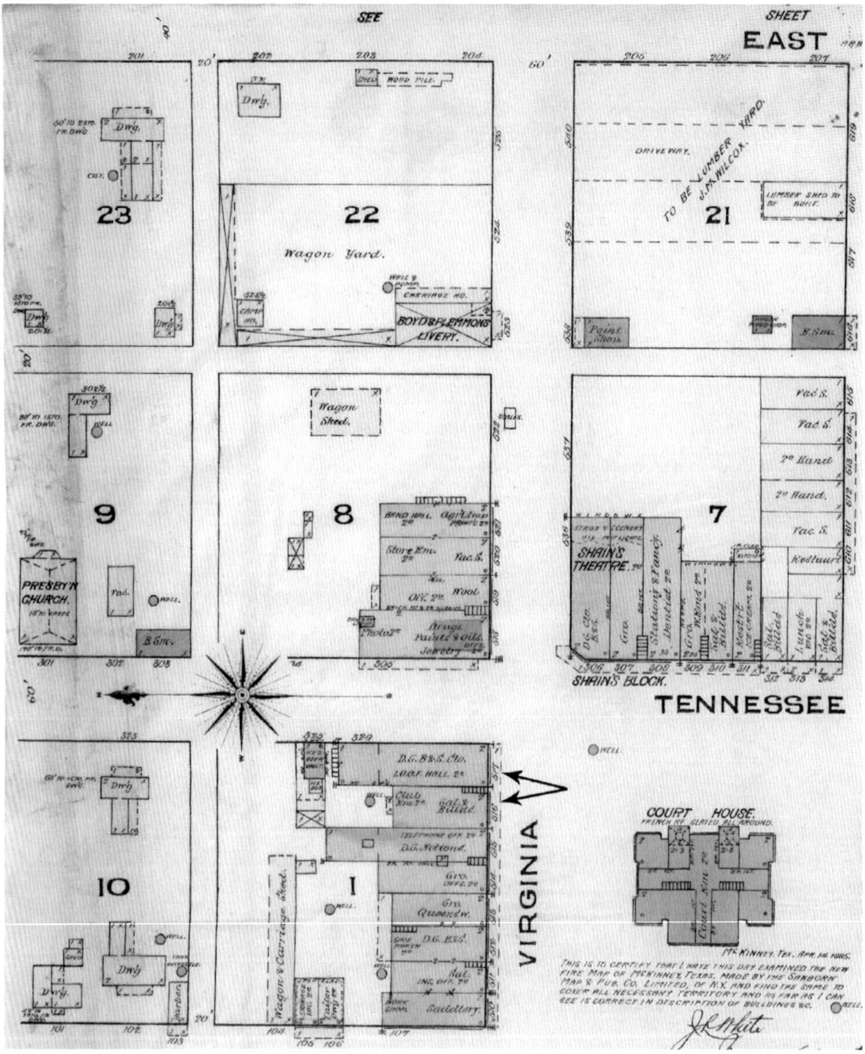


Sanborn Map of McKinney Square, 1885. On this map, the Odd Fellows and Bates buildings are located at the top of the corner of Virginia and Tennessee Streets. *Courtesy of the Briscoe Center for American History, University of Texas at Austin.*

A more significant expansion of the building came six years later with the addition of a third floor. In adding a third floor in 1891, the lodge was following a local trend. The Newsome Building, on the southeast corner of the square, added a third floor in 1891, as did the Belmont Hotel. A short article in the May 28 edition of the *Democrat* confirms the year of

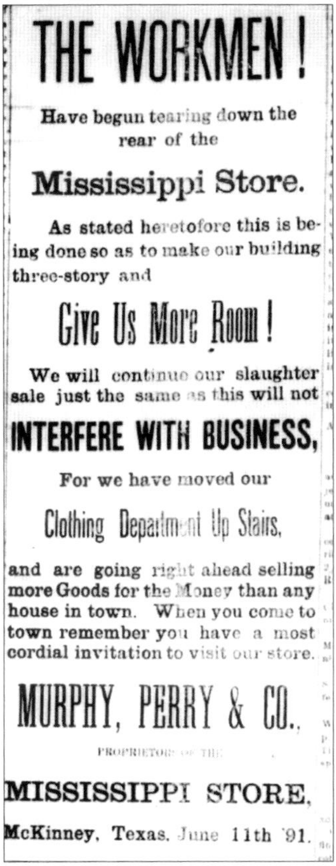


This local newspaper ad refers to the third-floor addition in 1891. *The* Democrat *(McKinney).*

the addition, stating that the Independent Order of Odd Fellows had let a contract for the third story and work was to begin at once.[17] Murphy, Perry & Company, which occupied the lower floor at that time, used the opportunity to launch and promote a big sale it claimed necessary to move inventory out of the way of construction efforts. The dry goods store continued using the building expansion as a theme in its advertising, informing customers on June 11 that construction was underway and inviting shoppers to see the enlarged quarters on September 24. The work had taken about fourteen weeks.

The architect on the project was William S. Sterrett of Dallas. Sterrett, who advertised his company, W. S. Sterrett & Company, as architects and superintendents, likely served as contractor.[18] Gideon Dowlen, a freelancing construction worker and longtime McKinney resident, also worked on the third-floor addition in 1891. When interviewed many years later, Dowlen claimed that Sterrett quit the job before it was complete but offered no explanation for Sterrett's departure, saying only that he (Dowlen) had finished the work.[19]

According to statements made by spokespersons for the Odd Fellows lodge, the addition was buttressed using iron columns set into six- and eight-inch wooden columns, with exterior walls measuring thirteen inches thick. There was apparently much discussion about adding the third floor and the building's capacity to accommodate the extra weight, but according to officers of the local Odd Fellows chapter, the architect made a thorough inspection and approved the addition.[20] With the work complete, the lodge moved to the newly constructed third floor, giving over the second-floor space to tenant Murphy, Perry & Company. For more than two decades, the business plan worked splendidly for the lodge, with the rental income used to pay down debt secured by a lien on the building.[21]

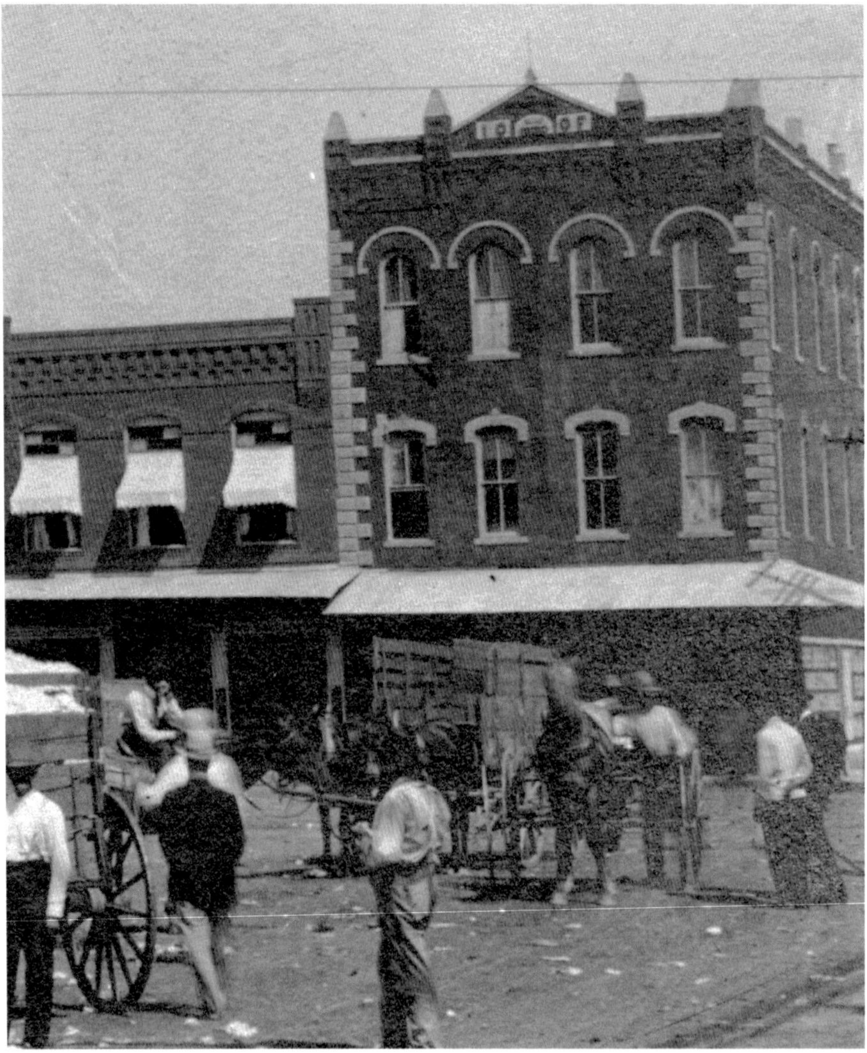

The stores as they looked after the third story was added to the Odd Fellows building. *Courtesy of McKinney Historic Preservation Office.*

For most, if not all of the years that the lodge sought commercial renters, dry goods stores occupied the lower levels of its building. The most enduring of those establishments, founded in September 1887 and commonly called the Mississippi Store, had an interesting lineage that revolved around a Mississippi transplant named George Stuart Murphy. As mentioned, the Mississippi Store began as Murphy, Perry and Company's Mississippi Store,

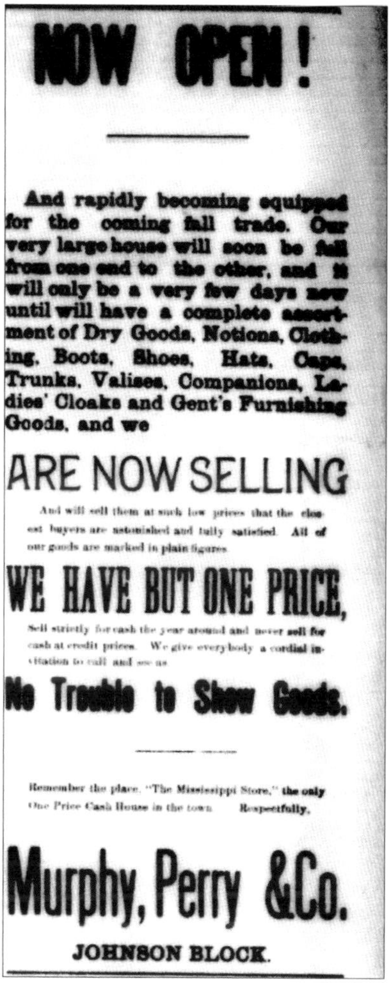


This ad, which ran on September 8, 1887, announces the opening of the Mississippi Store. *The* Weekly Democrat-Gazette *(McKinney)*.

the creation of George Murphy, who was thirty-five in 1887, and his twenty-nine-year-old brother-in-law, Thomas Cate "T.C." Perry.[22] Among the Mississippi Store's early employees was a young man named James Robert "J.R." Joiner. Joiner soon became a member of management as well as a member of the family when he married George Murphy's daughter Mattie in 1889. Joiner also partnered in a store his father-in-law owned in Sherman, forming Murphy, Joiner and Company.[23]

The Mississippi Store operated under the Murphy/Perry banner for six years, including the year(s) of the building expansion, but in December 1893, J.R. Joiner and T.C. Perry announced that they were forming a new company: Joiner, Perry and Company. The change was to be effective

February 1, 1894, but for reasons unknown, the Perry/Joiner proposal never materialized. Instead, in March 1894, the company ownership experienced a complete reversal when it reverted back to a sole ownership by Murphy. George Murphy & Company operated for a few months before Murphy's name again disappeared, replaced by T.C. Perry and a new partner, Lemuel Oldham. George Murphy moved to Sherman, opening another store in Bonham and Sulphur Springs, but remained close to T.C. Perry, his former associate/brother-in-law.[24]

Back in McKinney, Perry, Oldham and Company, still operating as the Mississippi Store, was struggling—the situation so critical that after a little more than a year, the partners were forced to declared bankruptcy. Soon after the insolvency, T.C. Perry moved to Fort Worth, and Lemuel Oldham moved to Mississippi. On January 13, 1897, a judge appointed Ben Estes, a longtime employee of the store, trustee of the establishment's remaining assets. On February 4, Estes presided over a private sale at which he solicited bids on the remaining merchandise.[25] McKinney's Racket Store, located on the southeast corner of the square and owned by William A. Purnell, submitted the winning bid.

The Racket Store moniker was not just a name—it was a concept—and was not unique to William Purnell. The name was a generic one commonly used for variety stores featuring discounted merchandise—the equivalent of today's dollar stores—meaning most towns had at least one such store. McKinney's version began in 1891, when Jerry E. Talbert opened a Racket Store on South Virginia Street, next to the post office. The store was so small that competitors reportedly tagged it the "hen coop."[26] The slur proved useless in discouraging customers, and by the end of 1895, Talbert was inclined to seek larger quarters on the square and invite an employee, William Purnell, to be his partner. In September of the following year, Talbert, who was considerably older than Purnell, retired due to failing health. Purnell continued the Racket Store, often securing inventory by procuring the remaining inventory of failed businesses.

Soon after Purnell bought out the stock of the defunct Perry and Oldham Mississippi Store in early 1897, George Murphy reappeared to reclaim the location and the popular store name. Murphy, who was then successfully operating a store in Sherman as well as a store in Sulphur Springs, decided to close his Sulphur Springs store and move the inventory to McKinney to reestablish the Mississippi Store. Before Murphy moved in, the Odd Fellows refurbished the building slightly, installing new floors. Murphy, for the third time in a decade, opened the Mississippi Store in the same location, on

February 20, 1897, with the help of friend/employee Ben Estes. The venture was short-lived, however. Within a few months, Murphy decided it best to concentrate his efforts on his store in Sherman. He sold the entire business, including the store name, to William Purnell in December 1897 for $30,000, finally ending his sporadic relationship with McKinney's Mississippi Store. In early March 1898, Purnell closed his Racket Store and moved into the Odd Fellow's building, where he became the newest owner/operator of the eleven-year-old Mississippi Store.

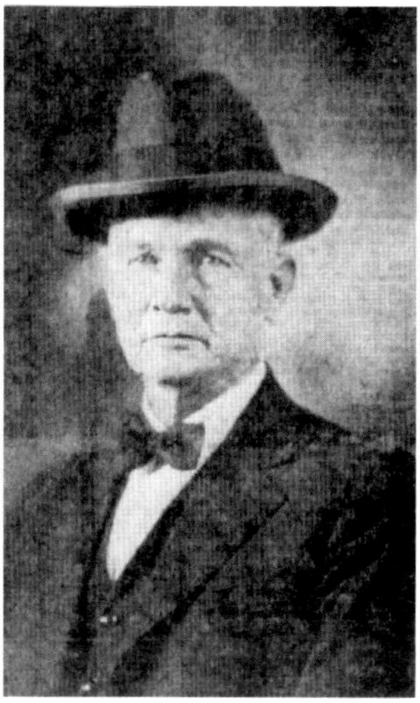

Thomas A. Cheeves, founder of Cheeves Bros. stores. *From an unknown newspaper, image provided by Kevin McCulloch.*

William Purnell operated the Mississippi Store for six years after he purchased it from George Murphy, with apparent success, but he was also involved in other business prospects in New York. In 1903, when he heard that the well-known Cheeves Brothers enterprise was considering adding a store in McKinney, he seized the opportunity and entered into negotiations with Thomas Cheeves to sell his store. The clever Cheeves brothers were in a position to capitalize on the recent closings of two of McKinney's oldest general stores, Newsome's and Aron and Alexander, establishments that predated the Civil War. Thomas Cheeves and William Purnell struck a bargain, and the sale was soon consummated, closing in late January 1903, the price not disclosed.[27] Purnell's most recent lease with the Odd Fellows organization, which he assigned to Cheeves as part of the sale, was good until the last day of 1912. Purnell moved his family to Greenville, Texas, and later to Brooklyn, New York.

The new owners of the McKinney store were brothers Thomas and Whitfield "Whitt" Cheeves and an associate named J.B.E. Brown. The store opened under its modified name, Cheeves Bros., Mississippi Store, on Monday, February 9, 1903, the company's tenth store. Other locations at that time were in Marlin, Corsicana, Tyler, Waxahachie, Temple, Mexia, Killeen, Calvert and Cameron.

The citizens of McKinney welcomed the Cheeves franchise. The local paper characterized the sale as "the biggest deal in business circles so far of the new year."[28] That statement, if examined closely, is rather comical—because the sale occurred in January—but there is no reason to believe that the sentiment was anything less than genuine. The Cheeves name was familiar and respected in Texas, its theme one of quality, polish and refinement, but the true test of acceptance was measured by patronage, a test that the Cheeves store soon passed.

Cheeves remained in the leased space, keeping much of the Mississippi Store staff and establishing J.B.E. Brown as manager. For reasons unknown, in September, after spending only a few months as part owner and manager, Brown sold his interest in the store to the other partners and moved to Fort Worth. Whitt Cheeves, who lived in Cameron, managed the McKinney store until he settled on a new manager. Drawing, as they often did, from the ranks of family members, the Cheeves brothers enlisted Oscar C. Stewart, a brother-in-law of Whitt Cheeves, as the new manager. Stewart was the eldest brother of Carrie Cheeves, Whitfield's wife. He was promoted from his job as salesman in the Cheeves store in Temple and vested his interest by buying into the McKinney partnership.

By 1913, the Cheeves Brothers store had been operating profitably on the northeast corner of the square for a decade. The building had seen few changes over those years apart from the new floors added in 1897. In 1904, a plaster ceiling on the first floor was removed and replaced with a metal one. In 1912, new coats of paint freshened appearances. Although the Cheeves brothers laid claim to more than a dozen stores that bore their family name, they never tried to distance themselves from the Mississippi Store's legacy in McKinney, wisely capitalizing on the store's popularity and longevity by keeping the name and the location. It allowed them to tout the store as the oldest in McKinney, despite the store's long string of ownership changes. It seemed a wise choice.

# 3

# THE TURBITT/BATES BUILDING

Peter Turbitt and James Ware chose a tough field when they entered the saloon business in McKinney. The number of saloons was plentiful, even though public sentiment about alcohol was decidedly mixed. In 1890, a list of saloons in McKinney numbered eight, including that of Peter Turbitt.[29] The situation mirrored that in many Texas towns, where objections to saloons ran high but so did patronage, with the more fervent opinions originating from the dry side of the divide. Many of those who objected to alcohol extended their resentment to property owners who rented to saloonkeepers, a sentiment that put men like Turbitt under double pressure. In McKinney, it appears that locals were almost evenly split on the subject in those early days, a situation that saw the town's collective opinion vacillate back and forth. In late March 1895, the town voted in favor of local prohibition, but just two years later, a vote taken on March 31, 1897, ended in victory for the saloons. In early March 1902, when Collin County voted to prohibit alcohol countywide, the Town of McKinney voted contrary to the county majority—hoping to keep its saloons. Peter Turbitt's saloons predated local option election laws, but his businesses did not escape public scrutiny and criticism from a contingent of locals, mostly religious leaders, who kept a constant campaign going against "demon rum."

It is more difficult to compile a comprehensive list of tenants for Turbitt's building than it was for the lodge building, perhaps because saloons did not receive the same level of exposure in newspapers that other businesses enjoyed. After Peter Turbitt replaced his burned-out building in 1876, he rented the new brick building to another pair of saloonkeepers while he and James Ware embarked on a new line of business at a location nearby. The new enterprise was Turbitt & Ware, Ice Dealers, a company that not only delivered ice to homes but also embraced its role as an agent for the Anheuser Busch Brewing Company.[30] The icehouse, which was sometimes referred to as a grocery store with a billiards hall in the back, was located at 325 Tennessee Street, just behind the Mississippi Store. Early Sanborn maps show a large ice vault took up much of the building's interior (see the map on page 20).

While Turbitt and Ware sold ice, two brothers from Dallas named William and James Skelton reestablished the Parlor Saloon in Turbitt's new building. The brothers were widely known saloonkeepers in Central Texas and owned saloons in nearby Plano and Dallas. For reasons unknown, in late 1885, Peter Turbitt sought a buyer for his saloon building.[31] A local man named Bates answered the ad.

Constantine Dixon Bates, hereafter C.D. Bates, accomplished much during his life, considering the fact that he did not live to reach his fortieth birthday. Bates was born in Tennessee on February 27, 1849, but after the death of his mother in 1872, C.D., along with his siblings and father, John Henry Bates, moved to Texas. A smart and energetic young man, Bates quickly found success through hard work. He began working as a grocer but soon moved to the more lucrative trade of brokering cotton. Beginning in 1882, as many astute businessmen did, Bates invested his profits in real estate with the purchase of an attractive home, which had local women speculating that he was about to marry. The rumors proved true when Bates traveled to Tennessee in August 1883 and returned with his twenty-five-year-old bride, Lenora "Lea" Harris Bates.[32] Lea was the sister of another prominent McKinney resident, Plummer Harris.

In March 1883, shortly before he left for a trip to Tennessee, Bates announced that he was about to begin construction of a building on the east side of the square on Tennessee Street, along a row of commercial buildings known to locals as the Shain block. The block was named for Jesse Shain, an early builder and merchant in McKinney. Bates had acquired his property in the Shain block, lot no. 53 and a portion of lot no. 54, from G.A. Foote on January 31, 1882.[33] His commercial real estate holdings also included a warehouse and a small rent house, the latter located behind his home.

On December 30, 1885, C.D. Bates expanded his holdings in commercial property by purchasing Turbitt's saloon building on lot no. 7 on the north side of the square, as well as lots no. 1 and no. 2 on the same block. Bates paid Peter and Alice Turbit (spelling as it appears on the deed) $8,000 for the real estate, putting down $3,000 and signing promissory notes for the balance. The notes carried a staggering 12 percent interest rate. Interestingly, the deed records specifically mention the shared east wall as being a "party" wall belonging equally to Turbitt's building and Empire Lodge No. 68. The record also revealed another point of interest. The Turbitt Building had *two* shared walls. At the time of the fire of 1875, Turbitt's commercial neighbor to his immediate west was a store named Seay and Seay, a book and stationery store that rented space from Russell DeArmond, an attorney for the Houston and Texas Central Railway. The deed clearly states that Turbitt owned only half of his west wall, with the other half belonging to DeArmond.[34]

At the time the building was sold to Bates, the Skelton brothers were still in possession of the lower floor under a lease that ran until February 1, 1888. The deed referenced the lease agreement, stating that as long as the Skeltons paid the $100 per month rent, they could stay until the lease expired. Over time, the building became known as the Bates Building.

As late as 1892, the lower level of the Bates Building was still serving as the Parlor Saloon, although it is unclear who operated the business.[35] The local election of 1895, which put a two-year halt on the sale of alcohol, meant that the old saloon building had to be repurposed. A drugstore soon took possession. A series of photographers rented the upstairs space over a period spanning two decades. Those tenants, including George Wakely, W.F. Cobb, William Pennington and Spencer Smith, referred to their studios as photography galleries in those early days. At least one old picture of the Bates Building shows the word *gallery* painted in large letters across the front.

C.D. and Lea Bates had enjoyed a five-year marriage that produced two daughters when C.D. Bates suddenly died on June 20, 1888, of an illness his death notice identified as "congestion of the bowels."[36] It was a sad ending for a father and husband just thirty-nine years old. Although he left no will, Bates had purchased an insurance policy that paid his widow $5,000, a handsome sum in 1888. Lea Bates wisely used the money to pay down the debts against the leveraged commercial property. Lea Bates asked her father-in-law, John Henry Bates, to administer her husband's rather complicated estate, which he did. At the time of his death, C.D. was still receiving rent of $100 per month for the old Turbitt saloon building on the north side of the square. Probate records show the value of that building, including lots 1, 2, and 7, was placed at $8,500, while the value of the commercial building (including the lot) on the east side of the square was placed at $7,000.[37]

Some months after her husband's death, Lea, who was pregnant, returned to Tennessee with her daughters Mary and Nell, leaving her brother Plummer Harris in charge of managing the Bates properties. She gave birth to a son, the namesake of his father, on January 19, 1889. Lea remained in Nashville until her death.

In 1902, Plummer Harris enlarged the old saloon building on behalf of his sister, adding another fifty feet to the back of the building. The addition covered an old well and eliminated a large alleyway/yard behind the structure. The other Bates building, located on the east side of the square known as the Shain block, was destroyed by fire in 1904 along with several others on the same block. Harris, with his sister's permission, entered into an agreement with the owner of the property next door, J.L. Lovejoy, to replace the two burned buildings with one larger one. The result was a new, red brick, modern structure with a row of arched windows across the front. Lovejoy's former tenant, a popular drugstore known as Smith Brothers and Company, rented both floors of the new building. The old store name still adorns the exterior walls.

In April 1908, Lea sold the Bates family home that C.D. had purchased in 1882 in anticipation of their marriage. The buyer was L.A. Scott, and the sales price was $2,500.[38] Two years later, in early June 1910, Plummer Harris received word that Lea, who was fifty-two, had died. Oddly, the cause of death entered on Lea's death certificate was "exhaustion." Her children sent her body to Collin County, where she was laid to rest next to her husband. The couple had been separated by death twenty-two years earlier.

The ownership of the Bates property was split between the three Bates children, who were by then young adults. Less than two years after their mother's death, Nell Bates Allan, Mary Bates Gibson and Constantine Bates Jr. sold lot no. 53 and the portion of lot no. 54 they owned on the east side of the square to the First National Bank of McKinney for the sum of $8,000.[39] They retained only the Bates Building, located on the north side of the square next to the Mississippi Store.

Perhaps the Bates children kept the building next to the Mississippi because it had provided steady rental income for so many years without fail. One tenant of long standing was A.G. Chandler, who operated a dry goods store in the Bates Building that later shifted its line to ladies wear. For several years, Chandler had operated in partnership with a man named Joe Armstrong. In March 1908, Chandler, who was suffering from poor health, sold the business to Frank W. Emerson, who kept the enterprise in the same location until 1910.

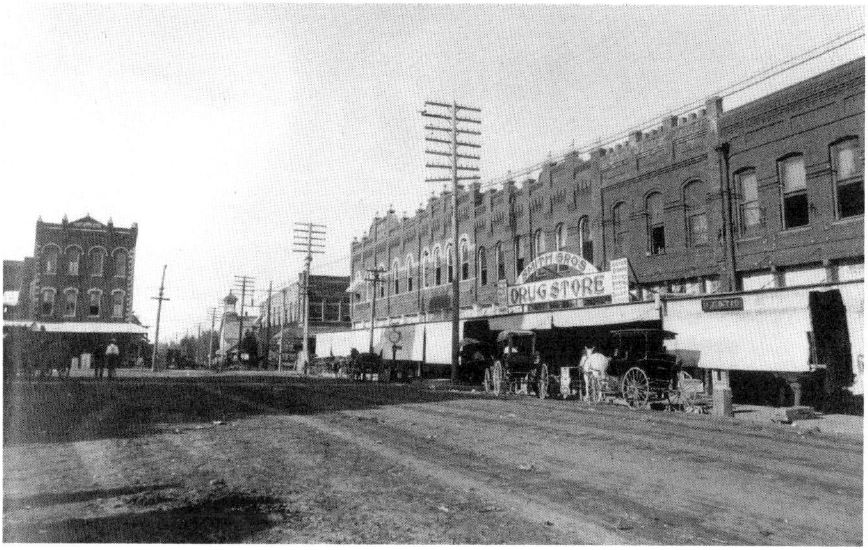


The Smith Drug Store prior to the 1904 fire. *Courtesy of McKinney Historical Preservation Office.*

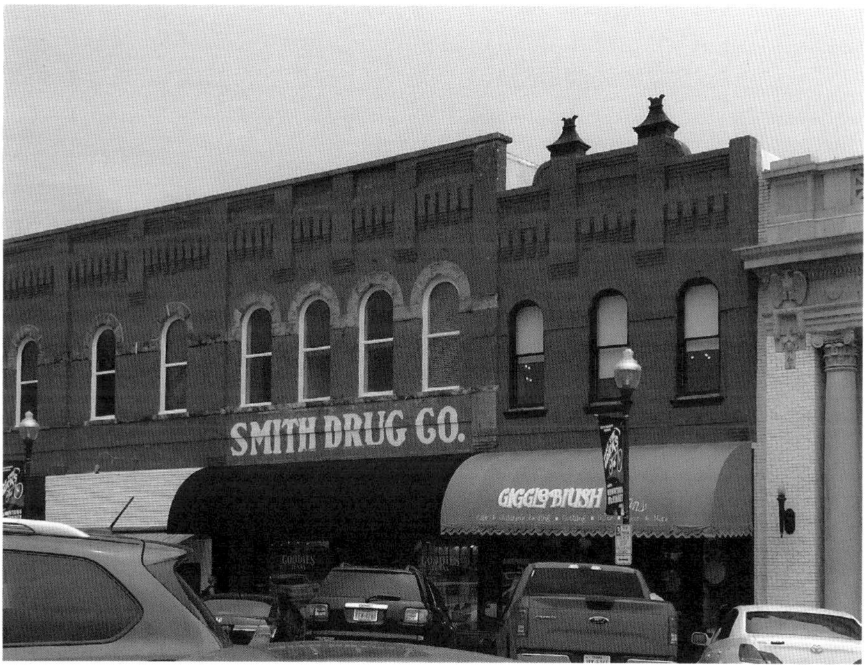


The iconic Smith Drug building as it appears today. *Author's collection.*

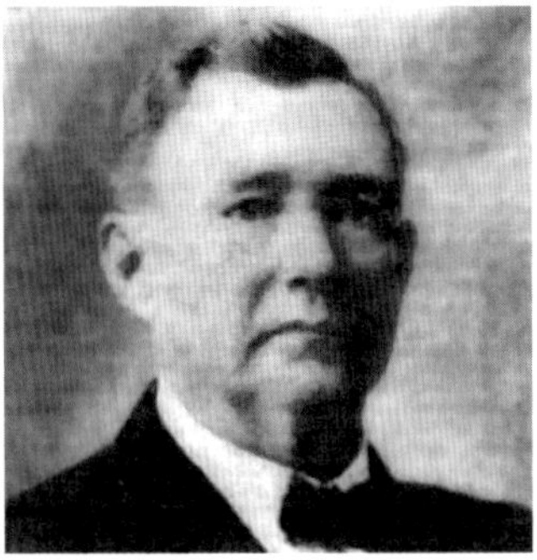

Thomas J. Tingle, the "Implement Man." *The* Weekly Democrat-Gazette *(McKinney)*.

The renter of the Bates Building in 1913, fifty-two-year-old Thomas Jefferson Tingle, was a relative newcomer to McKinney. Tingle, who advertised himself as the "Implement Man," moved to McKinney in 1911 from Childress, Texas. He rented both floors of the building, operating his farm implements store on the lower level and using the upper floor for storage. His lease, drawn up by Plummer Harris, began on October 1, 1911, and covered a period of three years. It required him to pay $1,000 per year in rent, payable in monthly installments.[40] Tingle heavily advertised, showcasing the popular implements he carried in the B.F. Avery line. To facilitate lifting bulky and weighty objects to the upper level, Tingle installed a lift and new stairway. With shared walls on both sides of the building, there were few windows, prompting Tingle to also install a skylight.

In 1913, the owners of the Bates and lodge buildings likely considered themselves lucky. With Tingle Implements and the Cheeves Mississippi store as reliable tenants, it appeared that they had few concerns regarding their well-located properties. They had been spared three fires on the square subsequent to the fire of 1875, including one in 1887 that destroyed fifteen businesses, and a 1904 blaze that took out half of the structures on the east side. Destruction by fire was a fairly common occurrence in those early days; what happened on January 23, 1913, was not.

# 4
# THE CHEEVES FAITHFUL

By 1913, the Cheeves store in McKinney had been flourishing for a decade under the capable leadership of manager Oscar Stewart and the equally capable work of other workers, many of them longtime Mississippi Store employees. Stewart, who grew up in Falls County, Texas, had moved to Cameron and then to Temple sometime prior to 1900. He learned the dry goods business working as a salesman in the Temple Cheeves store while living with Carrie and Whitt Cheeves, his sister and brother-in-law. Those living arrangements suggest that the Cheeves brothers were likely grooming Stewart for a position in management that would require him to relocate. The move to McKinney, made in 1903 when he was thirty, proved a good choice for Stewart. He was successful at managing the Cheeves store and equally successful in finding a companion. In early March 1908, Stewart married Annie Taylor, the daughter of Captain W.H. Taylor, a former Collin County treasurer. Stewart was active in civic affairs, including the Elks lodge and the board of trade, a precursor to today's chamber of commerce. He traveled frequently and for long periods, going to market in St. Louis at least twice annually. On the afternoon of the fatal collapse, he was absent from the store, conducting business in Dallas.

A full staff at McKinney's Cheeves store consisted of about ten people, including the manager, but not the part-time delivery boys.[41] On the afternoon of the fatal collapse, eight regular employees were working as well as a delivery boy and a porter, who were inside the building when it collapsed. With so many dry goods stores located on McKinney's square, customer service was a critical element in ensuring that shoppers had a pleasant experience, and the clerks at Cheeves were keenly aware of that fact.

In 1913, Cheeves's most tenured and senior employee was seventy-two-year-old Ben Estes, a veteran of the original Mississippi Store and a man who seemed always to have had an expanded role at the store. For example, his name was on the lease during the years that William Purnell owned the store. Although Estes could boast of employment at the Mississippi Store that spanned twenty-six years in 1913, he held greater experience as the past owner of his own dry goods and grocery establishments. After the Civil War, young Ben had entered the dry goods business with a partner, forming Howell & Estes, later swapping one man named Howell for another of the same last name and, later still, for a new partner named Barry. The Estes & Barry partnership lasted until the great fire of June 27, 1875, consumed the store. It was the same fire that leveled Turbitt and Ware's Parlor Saloon, the original Odd Fellows building and ten other businesses. Estes moved to Sherman and then Brenham, where he lived for a short time, and where he may have met George Murphy. When Murphy and Perry opened their McKinney Mississippi Store in 1887, Estes returned to McKinney to work for them. Years later, when Perry, Oldham and Company went into bankruptcy, the judge entrusted Estes with the responsibility of trustee of the assets, a position he faithfully executed.[42]

Estes was described as a sensitive, tenderhearted man of integrity and solid character who made a habit of attending funerals of the poor and friendless. On the occasion of his seventy-seventh birthday in early 1918, the *Weekly Democrat-Gazette* ran a lengthy tribute to his interesting life. Born in Kentucky in 1841, Estes came to Texas in March 1856. His first job in the McKinney area was plowing, for which he was compensated fifty cents a day. He attended school when he was able but had to abruptly abandon that luxury when the Civil War began. He fought at the Battle of Pea Ridge and several other skirmishes and was captured at Hatchie Bridge, Mississippi, but soon released.[43]

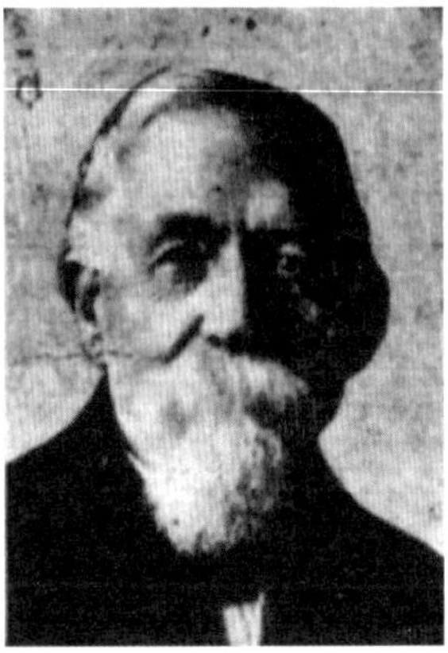

Ben Estes, a fixture in McKinney's early retail community. *The* Weekly Democrat-Gazette *(McKinney)*.

It is clear that the relationships between the employees at the store were close ones. Just three weeks before the accident in downtown

McKinney, Estes had buried his thirty-eight-year-old son, Dink, a victim of liver disease. To accommodate Ben and the other employees and as a show of respect, Oscar Stewart closed the store for two hours on the afternoon of the funeral. By 1913, Estes's advanced age kept him from working long hours, but he remained a fixture at the store and a knowledgeable addition to the staff. Ben worked in the store on the busy morning of January 23 but left the premises a short while before the buildings fell.

John Waller Thomas, a forty-nine-year-old salesman in 1913, was also among the higher-ranking employees at the Cheeves store. His service with the Mississippi Store went back to the Perry & Oldham years, when he had worked both as a salesman and a bookkeeper.[44] For his efforts, Thomas had been rewarded with a promotion to the position of manager of dress goods. He and his wife lived on South Parker Street, not far from the square.

The Thomas family had strong ties to the McKinney area. John's father, James Waller Thomas, came to Texas from Missouri in 1845, settling in McKinney in 1859, and he established the town's first newspaper, the *McKinney Messenger*. Thomas was a man of conviction who maintained his

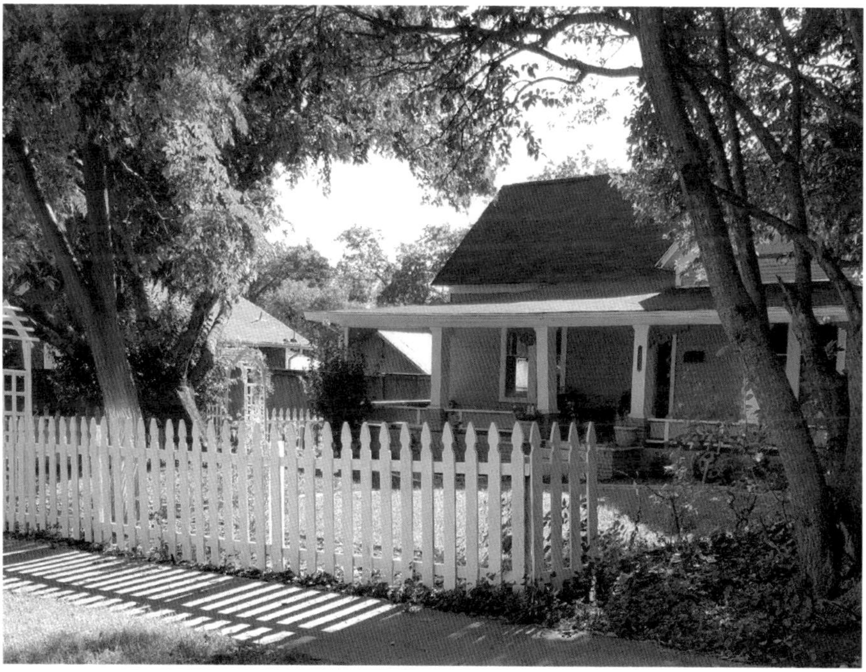

The John Thomas family home as it appears today. *Author's collection.*

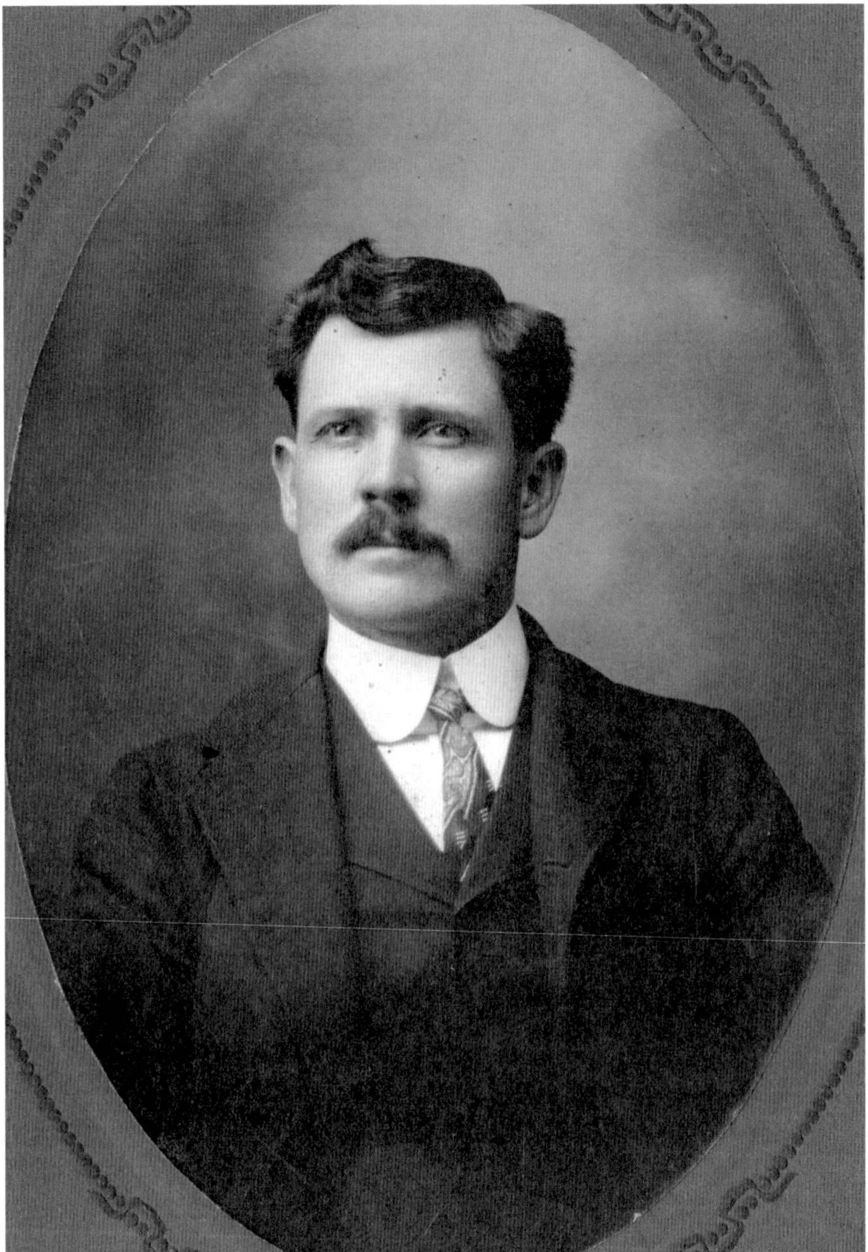

John Waller Thomas, a gentleman. *Courtesy of John Mack Thomas.*

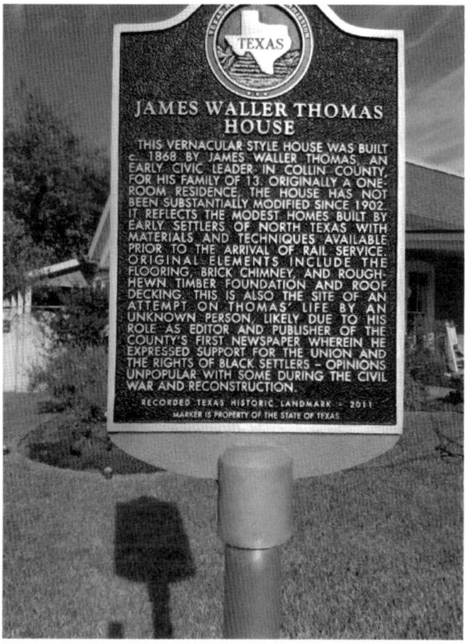


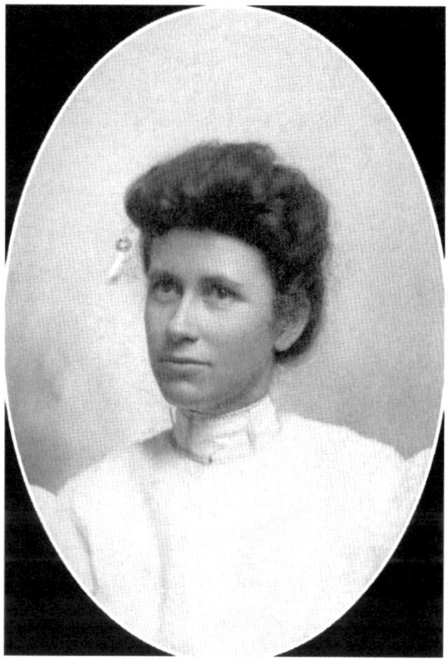

*Left*: Marker at James Thomas's home. *Author's collection.*

*Right*: Mary "Stella" Horn Thomas. *Courtesy of John Mack Thomas.*

allegiance to the Republican Party during the Civil War, a decision that was sometimes dangerous in the South. After leaving the newspaper business, James Thomas was McKinney's postmaster for many years. John was the second of eight children in the Thomas household, and his brother Jim, who played a minor role in this story, was the youngest. The brothers were close to each other in spirit and proximity as adults, the families living beside each other on South Parker Street. The James Thomas home, where the brothers grew up, is located on Benge Street and is easy to locate due to the historical marker that stands in front.

In 1892, John Thomas married Mary "Stella" Horn, the college-educated daughter of a popular local minister, Robert Cannon Horn. Elder Horn, a veteran of the Civil War, became a minister after the conflict was over. He officiated at many weddings and funerals in Collin County and kept a journal for sixty-five years, a valuable piece of Collin County's recorded history.

By 1913, the John Thomas family included two sons, Clifford and Russell, ages twenty and thirteen. By all accounts, John Thomas was a gentleman, a devoted family man and an active member of the community, and Stella was a tireless worker in the Christian Church.

Luther George Stephenson was the youngest member of the Cheeves staff and a part-timer. According to a notation made on a picture taken in his youth, he was sometimes called George and began working in 1908, when he was just twelve years old. Stephenson, one of eight children living on the Stephenson family farm, turned seventeen just one month before the accident. He worked for Cheeves as a delivery boy and had just returned to the store through the back door when the building began to quiver.

Fifty-two-year-old Belle McWilliams was a saleswoman at Cheeves, a widow, the mother of three grown children and one grandchild. By 1913, she had been working at the Mississippi Store for nineteen years, having also survived the Perry, Oldham bankruptcy. Belle was a spiritual woman of refinement whose proudest accomplishments included her three children, all young adults. Son John was a Presbyterian minister and son Roy was an employee of Wells Fargo and a McKinney fireman. Roy's name was among those listed as having saved half of the east side of the square in the fire of 1904 that destroyed several stores, including the eastside Bates Building. Belle also had a daughter named Annie Belle McKey. Annie Belle and the rest of the family had suffered much heartache over the preceding two years. In 1911, Annie Belle's husband James McKey, a young ticket agent for the railroad, died of pneumonia. In June the following year, Annie's twenty-one-month-old son, the namesake of his father, also died after a short illness. In 1913, Belle was sharing a beautiful home she had built in 1902 with her young widowed daughter and nine-year-old granddaughter, Rosebel.

On January 9, 1913, a local newspaper reported that Belle McWilliams was taking a vacation. The paper deemed the event newsworthy because it was her first vacation in nineteen years. "Mrs. Belle McWilliams, who has been one of Cheeves Bros. & Co.'s efficient salesladies for the past nineteen years, is taking a much needed vacation for the first time in this long period. Mrs. McWilliams is a splendid saleslady, and her many friends will miss her at the old Mississippi Store, and will be glad to see her back again after her vacation."[45] Mrs. McWilliams was just back from her break on the day of the collapse.

Lewis Vernon "Vernie" Graves was also considered a seasoned employee at the Mississippi Store. Like John Thomas, Ben Estes and Belle McWilliams, he could trace his years of work at the Mississippi Store to the days of Perry, Oldham and Company, and like Ben Estes, he seemed to have had a great deal invested in the business. His name, like that of Estes, was also on the store's lease during the Purnell years. Vernie was the proud son of Albert Goodwin Graves, a college-educated man who served as a captain

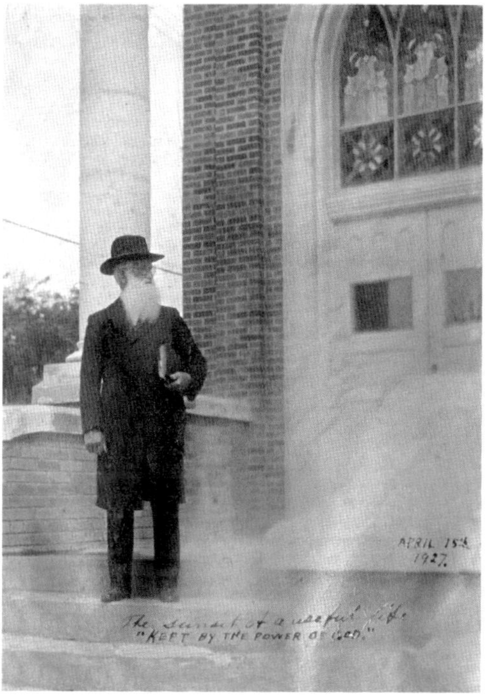


*Right*: Elder Robert Cannon Horn, Stella's father, on the steps of his church. *Courtesy of John Mack Thomas.*

*Below*: Luther Stephenson at about age thirteen. *Courtesy of Bess Miller.*

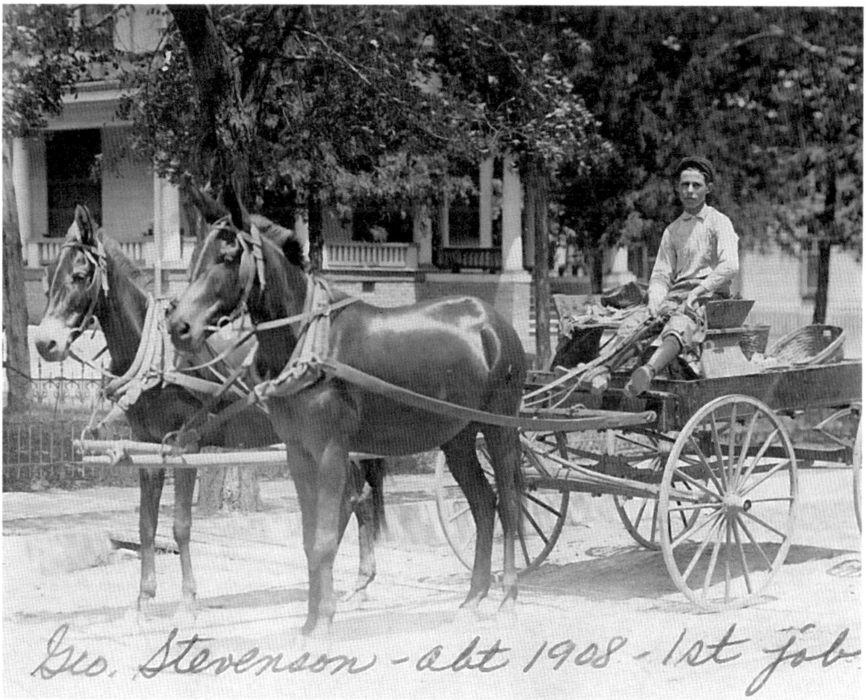

in Throckmorton's company during the war. Vernie Graves had spent many years learning the sales trade with an eye on one day opening his own business. In 1913, he was forty-one, married and the father of thirteen-year-old Virginia and eleven-year-old Lewis Jr.

Clerk Annie M. Curts was one month short of her twenty-fifth birthday and unmarried on the day the store fell. Her father, William S. Curts, was the chairman of the county's Republican Executive Committee. Annie was the youngest of six children and a studious young woman, her name often appearing in the local paper as a spelling champion and honor roll student. The Curts family moved from nearby Roland to McKinney in 1904, when Annie was a teen. Compared to some of her co-workers, Annie was a new hire at Cheeves, even though she had been working as a salesclerk and milliner at the store for at least three years in 1913.

Eva and Lula Searcy were sisters who worked at Cheeves. The young women were two of five daughters and two sons that comprised the Leonard H. Searcy Jr. family. Their father, who was known as Dick, was a farmer and the son of Leonard Harrison Searcy Sr., a Collin County pioneer. Before his death, the senior Searcy held the distinction of being one of the last early area residents to survive a bloody encounter with Indians. For many years, the Searcy family lived on a farm in Walnut Grove, moving to McKinney in 1902. The Searcy name was a common one in Collin County. Allen Searcy, a Collin County resident and a brother to Dick, was the father of six girls. Eva and Lula Searcy spent their lives surrounded by siblings and cousins, most of them females. Separated in age by eight years, sisters Eva and Lula were both at work when the disaster occurred; Eva, a saleswoman, was twenty-five, and Lula, a cashier, was thirty-three. Lula had previously worked at Bray Brothers Dry Goods—experience that likely helped her earn a position as cashier at the Cheeves store.

Mary Emerson Stiff was a twenty-seven-year-old single mother of two in early 1913, the youngest of eight Emerson children. Mary, the victim of a failed marriage to a man named Oliver Stiff, lived with her mother and two young sons in a small hotel/boardinghouse called Emerson House.

The Emerson name was well known in Collin County. Mary's father, Thomas H. Emerson, along with his brother Turner, joined their father, Francis, in a successful banking business. For many years, the family's private bank, which later became the First National Bank of McKinney, was McKinney's only bank. Thomas Emerson's family had seen its share of sorrow and conflict over the years, including a sad and shocking murder that took place in the Emerson home.

In June 1899, when Mary was just fourteen, her eldest brother, Darious, who was thirty, got into a squabble with his mother and his brother-in-law, a man named Leroy Anderson. Darious and his wife and four children lived a few houses away from his parents on South Kentucky Street. The quarrel between Darious and his mother was fairly minor, but the clash between the brothers-in-law had reached a dangerous level that included death threats, reportedly lodged from both sides. One June evening, Darious had gone to his parents' home to speak to his mother about some angry notes that had passed between the two houses. It seems that Darious and his wife often sent one of their children to the elder Emerson home with a note asking for groceries, a practice that was creating tension. The last request had prompted Mrs. Emerson to send the child back with a testy reply rather than the requested food.

Leroy Anderson was married to one of the Emerson daughters, Carrie, and the couple lived in the elder Emersons' home. When Darious arrived at the house, intending to speak with his mother, Anderson locked himself in a second-floor bedroom, apparently fearing that Darious had come to carry out an earlier death threat. Mrs. Emerson (Darious's mother) later testified that she had heard her son threaten to kill Anderson on a previous day. The fact that Darious had made a death threat was true; the notion that he had come to the house that evening to carry out the threat was not. He carried no weapon.

As Darious tried to open the bedroom door, Anderson fired through it, delivering a fatal shot. Because Darious was found to be unarmed, a good deal of suspicion fell on Anderson. He gave himself up to the authorities and was later tried in a high-profile trial that must have been painful for the family. Anderson was acquitted, but it was of little or no consolation. In addition to their personal loss, the Emerson family had been forced to endure the indignity of having personal problems put on public display.[46]

Two years after her brother's murder, Mary's father died, and the year following that, 1902, her brother Mack, twenty-three, died after a short illness. Making matters worse, Mary and her mother were away on an extended trip to California and Colorado when Mack died. By 1910, Mary and her mother and Mary's two young sons lived at Emerson House, their home turned boardinghouse, and Mary worked at Cheeves.

Robert Norman Presley, aged thirty-five in 1913, was a quiet and likable man with a good deal of retail experience. Born in Alabama, he came to Texas with his family while young, settling in Bowie. He was slender and handsome, distinguishable by his prominent ears and shock of curly hair

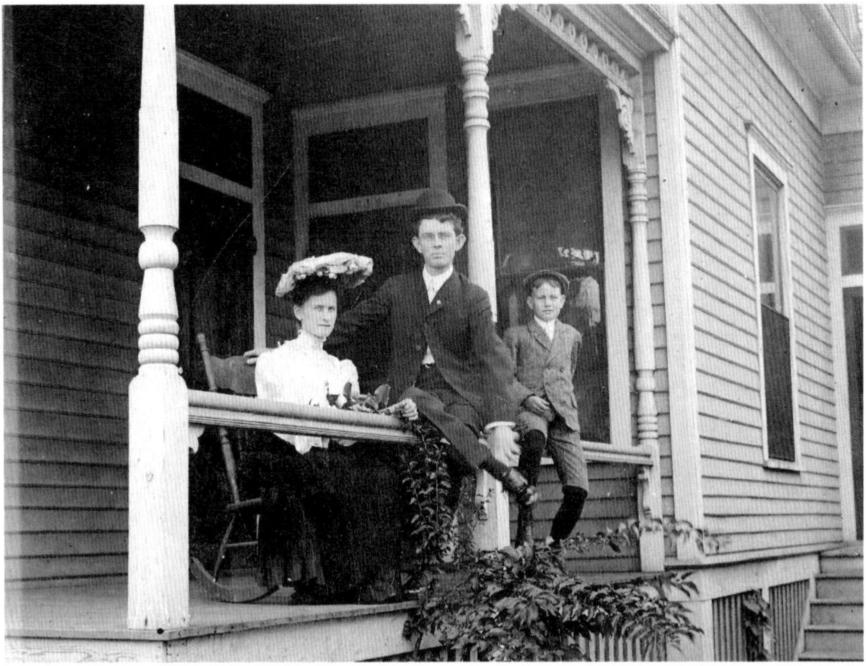

Norman and Sophia Presley and Sophia's young brother. *Courtesy of Robert M. Scott.*

that usually protruded beneath a hat. In 1900, when he was twenty-two and still living in Bowie, Norman, as he was called, was already working as a salesman. A Bowie resident named H.Z. Duke, who owned a chain of nickel stores in partnership with a man named Teal, hired young Presley to manage the company's McKinney store in early 1901. By June 1904, Presley had relocated to Dennison, where he worked for Bledsoe and Company, a racket store. In October 1904, he married Sophia Moore, the daughter of Lewis Moore, a longtime furniture merchant in McKinney. Sophia's sister Emma was a well-known milliner with the Mississippi Store, a career that began in 1898 and lasted fourteen years. Emma was highly respected in her field, so much so that she was allowed to travel to eastern markets to purchase inventory. Sophia had once worked with her sister at Cheeves, a job she began in September 1903 but left the following year when she married Norman Presley and moved to Dennison.

After a short stint in Sherman, where Presley continued to work as a manager of a racket store, he and Sophia returned to McKinney in August 1905. After a few years in the business, Norman believed he had gained enough experience to open his own store. He stayed within his area of

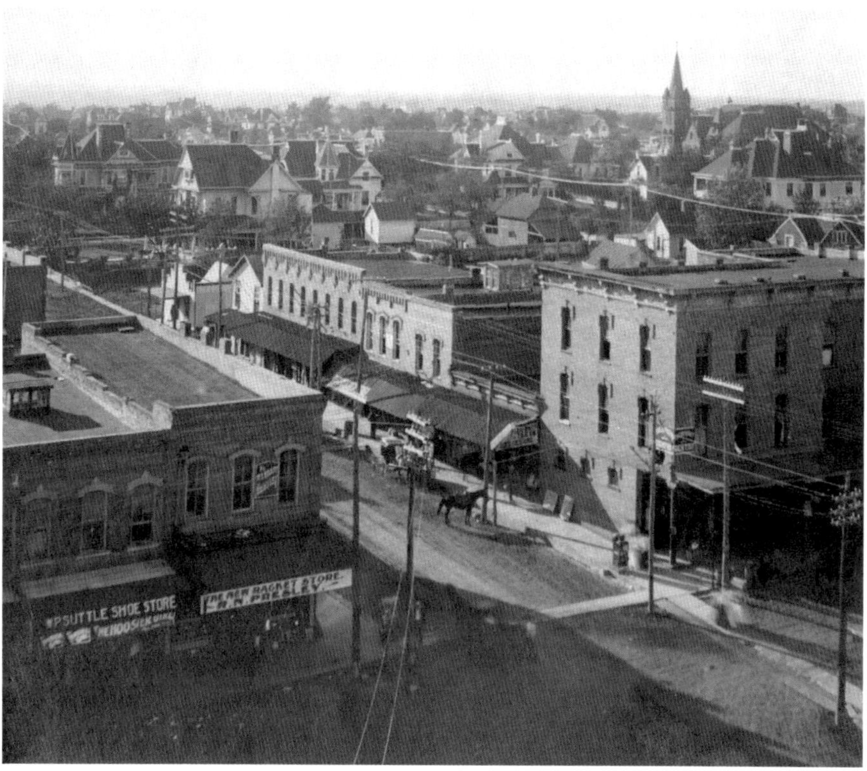


Presley's Racket Store (*second from bottom left*). *Courtesy of Collin County Historical Museum.*

expertise, opening a racket store on the northwest corner of the square in a building belonging to Jesse Shain on September 1, 1905. Presley put much time and energy into the operation, running frequent advertisements and offering free delivery, but unfortunately, after only a year of operation, he was compelled to file bankruptcy. The failure of his business was truly life-altering, yet the difference in Presley's assets and liabilities at the time he closed his store was a mere $300.[47]

After his failed attempt at operating his own store, Norman Presley went to work for Scott & Newsome, a store on the east side of the square. The establishment, which specialized in jewelry and books, closed about 1910. For a short time, Presley worked as a newspaper agent, but in early 1912, he obtained a sales job at the Cheeves store. It was a good match, Cheeves benefiting from Presley's experience and the young Presley family gaining a stable income. That element had become critical when Norman and Sophia welcomed a baby girl on November 23, 1911. They chose the name Emma

Lou, honoring Norman's mother, Emma Jane, his sister Emma Maude and Sophia's sister Emma Dora.

Norman Presley likely spent much of his workday on the second floor of Cheeves where the menswear was kept. The store was a long and narrow building with three-inch planked floors that ran lengthwise. A small office was located near the center of the first floor, and a storage room was located in the back, shared by the store and the Odd Fellows. Most merchandise was displayed in tall counters made of wood and glass. The back of the display cases slid open to enable clerks to easily retrieve items for customers requiring closer inspection. A wooden staircase led to the second floor, where clothing was displayed near the store's large millinery department.[48] On the lower floor and nearest the entrance, items of interest to female customers dominated the shelves and showcases. Shoes were located in the rear of the store. Two massive front doors were set back about five feet from the front façade, creating an alcove that was flanked by two large showcases, visible through large plate-glass windows.

As the Cheeves store readied to open its door on the morning of January 23, 1913, the scheduled sale on ladies' undergarments meant that two things were predictable: there would be a large number of female shoppers, and most would spend their time in the front of the store on the lower level. Nine members of the Cheeves staff took their places in anticipation of a demanding day. For some, it would be their last.

# 5
# A BROKEN CALM

The morning of Thursday, January 23, 1913, was a busy one in McKinney. The weather was clear but cold; a heavy rain, badly needed, had fallen overnight. Only five days earlier, a blue norther had swept into town, reminding residents that the season at hand was winter. With the holidays just over, retailers on McKinney's square knew that many shoppers needed inducements to coax them into stores. It was the peak time for the collection of property and poll taxes, when the tax collector placed reminders in the newspaper and extended his office hours to accommodate busy taxpayers.

On the south side of the square, in the Heard Building, a former opera house, clerks were busy filling shelves and assembling displays. A new branch of the Dallas-based Blair and Hughes grocery chain was being readied to meet a grand opening deadline of the first of February. The foundation for McKinney's new opera house was freshly laid, with contractors pushing toward a completion date three months hence. The First National Bank's new, heavily ornamented facility, located on the east side of the square, was within three weeks of occupancy.

As they had done each Thursday for seven years, owner/editors Tom W. Perkins and Walter B. Wilson of the *Weekly Democrat-Gazette* released their paper early on the morning of the twenty-third. The men, both well respected and popular, had been longtime competitors before 1906, when they pooled their journalistic talents and resources to the benefit of themselves and the community. Together, they produced the *Weekly Democrat-Gazette* as well as a daily publication, the *McKinney Courier-Gazette*. Tom Perkins was a born leader

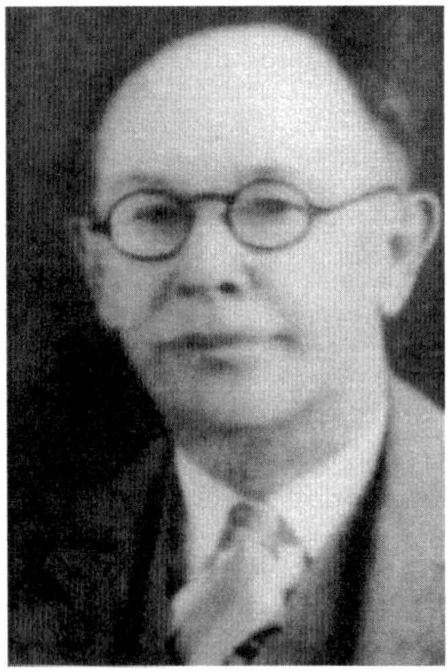

Walter B. Wilson. *The* Weekly Democrat-Gazette *(McKinney)*.

who served several nonconsecutive terms as McKinney's mayor and two terms as a state senator. Walter Wilson was the quintessential newsman, distinguished and recognizable in a pair of black, perfectly round rimmed spectacles. He kept fastidious notes and records and ended each day by logging brief notes about his life into a diary.

Events in McKinney during the preceding week had been routine, producing nothing worthy of a bold headline. A feature about McKinney's newly modernized steam laundry received front-page placement in the *Weekly*, as did a sketch of a proposed Baptist church. Notice of an upcoming banquet sponsored by the 'Possum and 'Tater Club also made the cut. Because McKinney was the county seat for Collin County, lists of grand jurors and newly filed lawsuits were standard fare in the weekly version of the *Gazette*. In the news-starved January 23 edition, they also qualified as front-page news.

Perhaps nothing reflects the character of a community more perfectly than its local newspaper, and so it was with the *Democrat-Gazette*. In 1913, life in McKinney was uncomplicated and inconspicuous. The character of the town had strayed little from that of its earliest days, with the biggest changes brought by steady growth. The population of the town, slightly fewer than five thousand in 1913, still consisted of groups of steady, fair-minded, hardworking, multigenerational families whose livelihoods were linked in some manner to farming or raising stock. Collectively, the people of McKinney could best be described as proud southerners and faithful Christians who looked out for one another.

While most of the features in the January 23 edition reflected a community with few pressing concerns, in retrospect, one story stands out as highly coincidental and somewhat prophetic. Its importance on the morning of the twenty-third might be measured by the fact that it was relegated to page eight. Headlined "Time Propitious for New School," the piece was almost certainly written by *Gazette* owner/editor Walter B. Wilson, a longtime member of the school board.[49] The editorial called for public support for a new city charter that would allow the sale of bonds to finance a new school. The thirty-nine-year-old Central Ward School building, one of McKinney's five overcrowded schoolhouses, was in critical need of replacement.[50] The situation was serious enough that the city superintendent had suspended the use of four classrooms on the south side of the building, citing the dubious integrity of the outer wall. Hoping to make a case it could present to the public, the school board sought professional assessments from a number of architects but failed to draw a full condemnation of the old building from any of them.

Still looking for solid proof that might garner public support, tenacious board members enlisted the expertise of John Stacke, a civil engineer who was considered among the best in the state. To their dismay, the expert opinions Stacke offered were not only vague but also outright contradictory. He assessed the building "safe" yet labeled the foundation faulty "to some extent," adding that a period of prolonged rain might threaten the structure. He declared that there was no immediate cause for alarm yet, when pressed to state whether it was advisable to use the building for another year, quickly answered "no." Paraphrasing, the editor of the *Gazette* included this troubling conclusion, which had been offered by the expert: "He assures the board that an old building, especially one as old as this one, would give ample warning in case it threatened to collapse."[51]

Members of the school board were certainly disappointed with the report rendered by the state's foremost authority. Using the expert's advise as a basis—and perhaps hoping to draw some public outrage—they placed the four rooms on the questionable south side of the building back into service and resumed their appeal for community backing. Walter Wilson could not have imagined that on the very day he published this plea, McKinney residents would learn the seriousness of the matter firsthand. Wilson, in his newspaper office just off the square, was among the first to reach the scene of the accident.

Taking up a much greater portion of space in the morning paper was an abundance of advertisements that beckoned shoppers to the square to partake of bargains. Mr. Tingle, the "Implement Man," tempted farmers by inviting them to join the Avery Burster Club. Membership required only that the customer purchase a plowing apparatus manufactured by the B.F. Avery Company. James Couch, the "Music Man," offered a variety of pianos in his store on Louisiana Street, including a used Steinway for just sixty-eight dollars.

But by far, the strongest marketing battles waged within the pages of the local paper were among McKinney's many dry goods establishments, where seasonal merchandise earned the greatest reductions. On January 23, J.H. Merritt, a dry goods store on the south side of the square, featured a full-

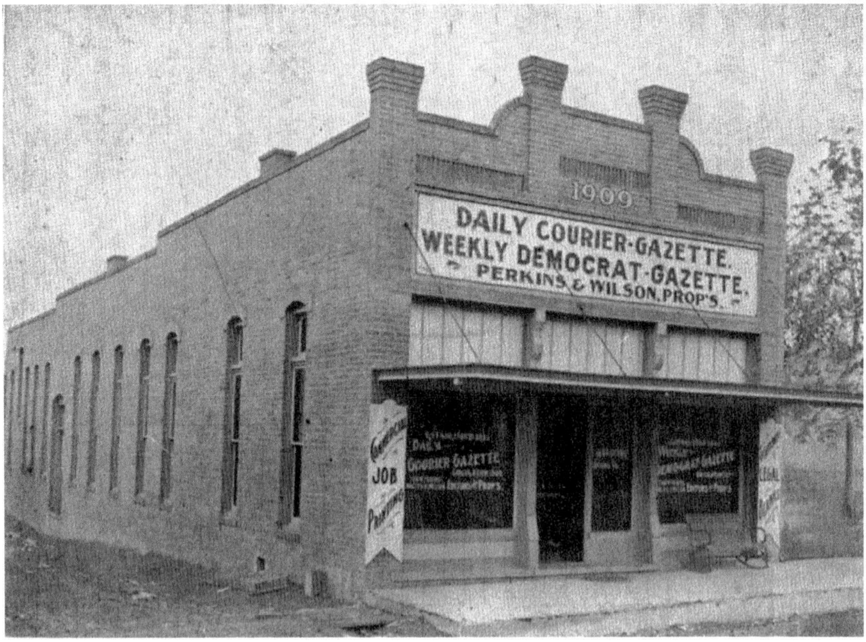


The home of the *Gazette. Reproduced from a photo in the 1914 high school annual for McKinney.*

page ad listing many samples of bargain prices. On the east side, Dick Allen's store promised huge savings on its winter stock of men's and boys' clothing. On the north side, Cheeves featured large markdowns on its inventory of ladies' undergarments, a sale it referred to as a "white sale." McKinney Dry Goods, which was situated catty-cornered from Cheeves on the east side of the square, was the most aggressive vendor. It offered tempting giveaways as incentives and engaged in other forms of hype. The clearance sale was scheduled to last ten days, and was so big that the store had closed on Tuesday to ready the merchandise and the staff for the extravaganza. Inducements included free dress patterns to the first twenty-five female shoppers and ten free yards of calico fabric to any lady spending one dollar or more. McKinney Dry Goods also offered to reimburse rail fare to any out-of-town shoppers who spent at least twenty-five dollars in the store. In addition to its sale items, the Matthew Brothers dry goods store advertised a newly installed elevator, inviting families to come in and let the children ride the only passenger elevator in town.

By all accounts, the various enticements worked, bringing many shoppers to the square that January morning. By midafternoon, however, activity was tapering off. Sometime around 3:30 p.m., the city marshal, who was also the fire chief of McKinney's volunteer fire department, John Sale McKinney, ambled into the McKinney Dry Goods store. His presence there would later be viewed as a stroke of luck. The slender, handsome, forty-five-year-old city officer was serving his ninth year as fire chief and seventh year as city marshal. John McKinney may have stopped at the dry goods to check on store manager J.H. Montgomery, who had recently returned to work after a near-fatal accident and a long recuperation period.

On the night of September 12, 1912, Montgomery had been lucky to survive electrocution while turning off a dropdown light in his home bathroom. He sustained a large, bone-deep burn to one of his thighs and layers of seared skin on his hands. His recovery period lasted eleven weeks, but Montgomery was still unable to attend to all of his duties, particularly bookkeeping and other functions that required him to write. John McKinney answered a fire call near Montgomery's house on the night of his accident and was later called to testify when Montgomery brought a suit of negligence against McKinney Ice, Light and Coal Company.[52]

To say that Chief McKinney was a genial and trusted member of the community would be an understatement. Although he was not a direct descendant of Collin McKinney, the namesake of the town and county, John nonetheless inherited a sound claim to any distinction due founding families. The chief's father, John Meyers McKinney, was a much-loved minister and farmer who came to Collin County as an adolescent in 1846; he claimed that he drove the first team of oxen to break ground in McKinney's fertile soil.[53] The elder McKinney's marriage in 1857 to Polly Ann Coffey, the daughter of another Collin County pioneer, further entitled the couple's six children, of which John S. was the fifth, to a level of pioneer family bragging rights.

Although John S. McKinney liked to indulge in stories about the early days in Collin County, he wasn't prone to bragging, nor did he need any aggrandizement to distinguish himself. He occasionally broke with that custom to boast about the unfailing watch he had carried for thirty-six years, but like his father, he was much loved and respected on his merits. In 1913, John was less than halfway through a career in public service that would span more than thirty years. In the earliest years, he had performed those services, as well as those of constable, without remuneration. Apart from his law enforcement and firefighting duties, Chief McKinney was a family man and father of four—a fixture at parades, banquets and other social events—a local favorite who earned admiration from his neighbors

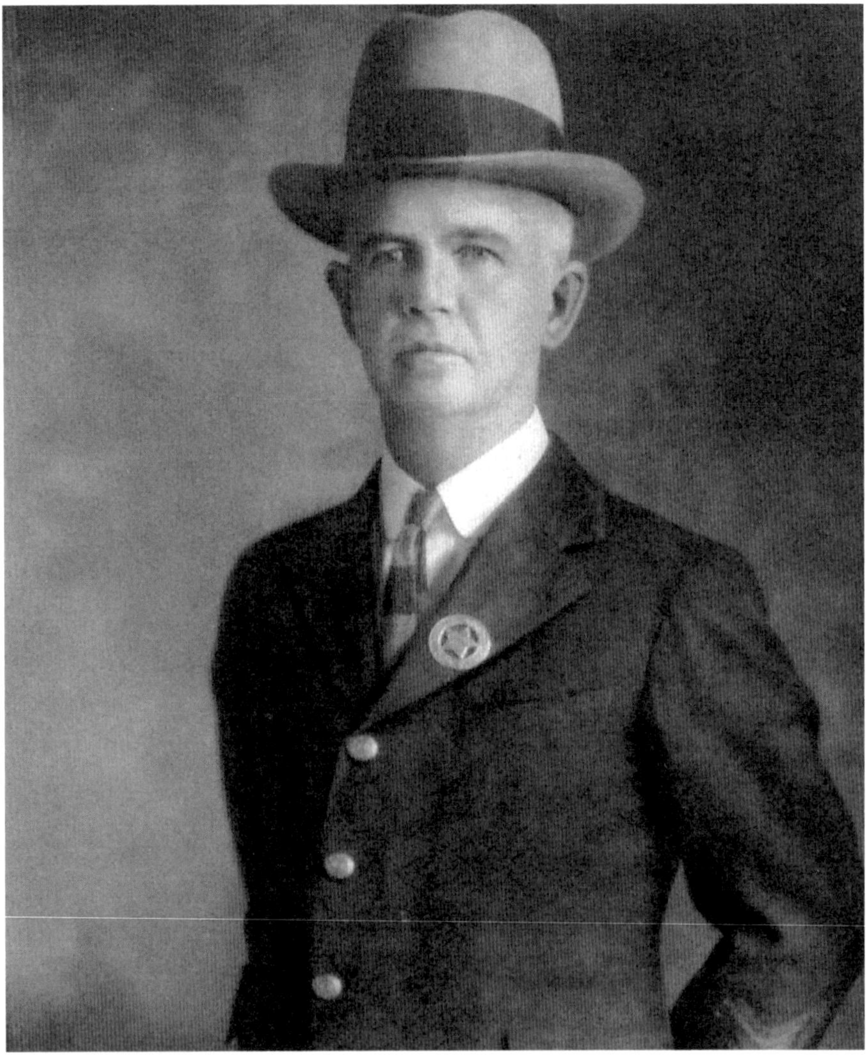

Chief John S. McKinney in later years. *Courtesy of Dirk Hedges of the McKinney Fire Department.*

and an affectionate nickname, "Uncle Johnny."[54] But John McKinney's best attribute was his ability to remain cool under pressure, a trait that allowed him to make measured decisions.

The earliest firefighters in McKinney, like those who battled the 1875 fire that destroyed the north side of the square, were untrained, and their firefighting efforts were yet to be organized. The first serious attempt to systematize firefighting efforts in McKinney came in 1887, when a few industrious men joined forces to form a group of trained volunteer firemen. Scattered efforts created two other teams of firemen, but fragments of those groups were later discontinued or consolidated into a single department.[55] The fire department grew and developed over time, securing a building and a fire bell that replaced the old pistol shot that had once served as an alarm. So many fires had occurred on the square, it was once common practice for several of the volunteer firemen to take turns spending the night in the courthouse.[56] McKinney's fire boys were appreciated and respected by the community, and men competed for the chance to fill openings when they occurred. The firemen reveled in the much-deserved praise—often parading their members and their fire wagon—and were frequently the honorees, and sometimes the hosts, of banquets and other events.

By early 1913, John McKinney had held authority over many men and scores of firefights. Most recently, on a Sunday afternoon just two weeks prior, the Owens Lumber Company had been spared by the efficient efforts of his volunteers. Two homes were lost, but the flying embers that floated to the nearby lumberyard were quickly and thoroughly extinguished. G.W. Owens, the owner of the lumberyard, made a fifty-dollar donation to the fire department in appreciation of those efforts, and Mrs. McAulay, whose home burned despite the men's best efforts, made a twenty-five-dollar donation.[57]

As he walked into McKinney Dry Goods midafternoon on January 23, John McKinney had no hint that his management and rescue skills were about to be rigorously tested. He had faced challenges—but this would be different. As McKinney visited employees and customers in the McKinney Dry Goods store, the backdrop to a tragedy was forming, and a defining moment in the city's history was approaching. For years to come, everyone in McKinney that afternoon remembered precisely where he or she had been at 3:40 p.m.

Next door to the Cheeves store, T.J. Tingle stood inside about twenty feet from the front of his business talking to customer H.J. Brown. Farther back in the store, Tingle employee Robert H. Cogburn was speaking with Josiah Hewett, a new hire working his first day. Cogburn's six-year-old son, Henry, had come to work with his father that day and was standing nearby. Just outside the Tingle store, George J.S. Walker, a harness maker, was passing. Walker was among a dozen or so people scattered outside in various locations around the public square.

Joe, the "Tamale Man," as locals affectingly called him, was a fixture on the northeast corner most days, where he peddled tamales from a handcart.

Joe, who was visually impaired, stepped away from his usual spot in front of the Cheeves store just moments before the collapse, fully expecting to return to his mobile business. Dr. Jonas Knight, a thirty-eight-year-old osteopath, was standing on the sidewalk not far from the Cheeves entrance. Al Bomar, an agent for the Magnolia Oil Company, stood in the doorway of the store. Cheeves customer Stella Russell of Farmersville, age nineteen, along with her four-year-old nephew, Russell Hight, had just exited Cheeves. Stella had likely taken the child shopping to give her older sister Lelia, who also had an infant son, a little assistance. Stella and Russell were positioned on the sidewalk, shaded by one of the store's broad awnings, when the telltale rumble began.

Across the square, forty-five year-old Dallas resident Samuel G. Banks, a traveling salesman in the employ of the Waples-Patter Company, was making sales calls in McKinney that day. He peddled groceries, a fact that may have saved his life. Banks had walked along the front of the Cheeves building no more than five minutes before it fell but, having no business inside, did not stop. He later told newspaper reporters that he was on an adjacent corner when he heard a rumble and saw the buildings sink into a pile of rubble. On the south side of the square, another Dallas-based traveling salesman, R.E. Best, was visiting with local grocer Jim Andrews when the two heard and

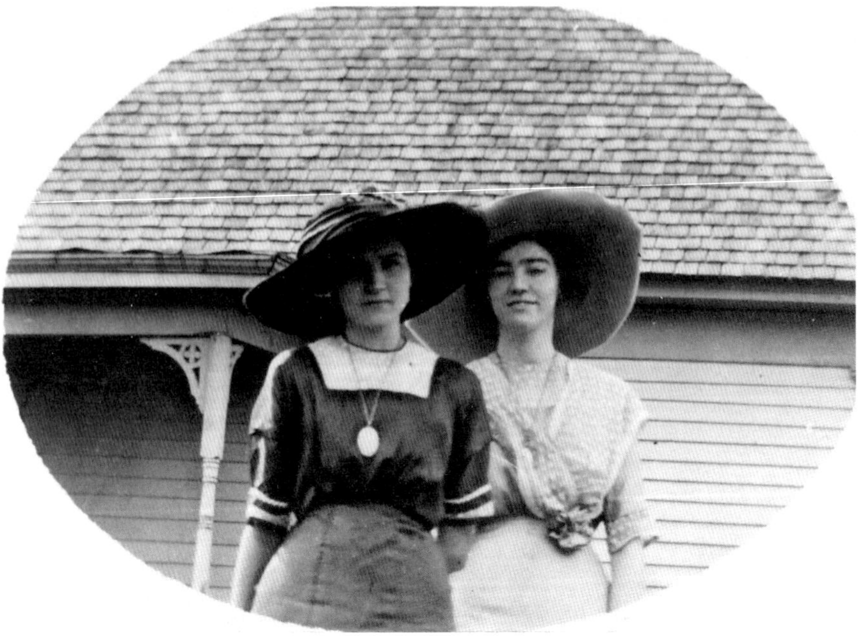

Stella Russell (*right*), with her sister Linnie. *Courtesy of Martha Prince.*

felt the reverberation that accompanied the collapse. James A. Waters, the proprietor of a shoe store located on the east side of the square, was standing outside talking to Walter D. Howell, his commercial neighbor. Howell was the co-owner of Howell & Lucas, a menswear store. The cover photo shows Waters shoe store on the far right; the Howell & Lucas store next door is just out of view.

At the center of the square, J.C. Moore stood in the doorway of the courthouse. Moore was a prosperous merchant, the longtime owner of an implement store on South Kentucky Street that likely represented T.J. Tingle's fiercest competition. It was coincidental that Moore witnessed the fall, because he had more than a casual interest in the Odd Fellows building. In 1891, when the third floor was added to the building, J.C. Moore represented the lodge in overseeing the construction. A farmer named G.W. Lockey (or Lackey) stood a few steps below Moore on the courthouse steps. Located across the street was James "Jim" Thomas Jr., a postal employee. Thomas had a personal interest in the Cheeves store; his brother, forty-nine-year-old John Thomas, was working inside.

S.G. Surratt, a popular young shoe salesman, was standing in the doorway of his employer, J.A. Waters' Shoes, when the buildings fell. The shoe store had been a neighbor to Norman Presley's racket store years before. As he stood there, Surratt had no idea that in a matter of minutes, he would abandon his post to frantically search for survivors. He also had no idea that he would soon be serving as a pallbearer for a dear friend.

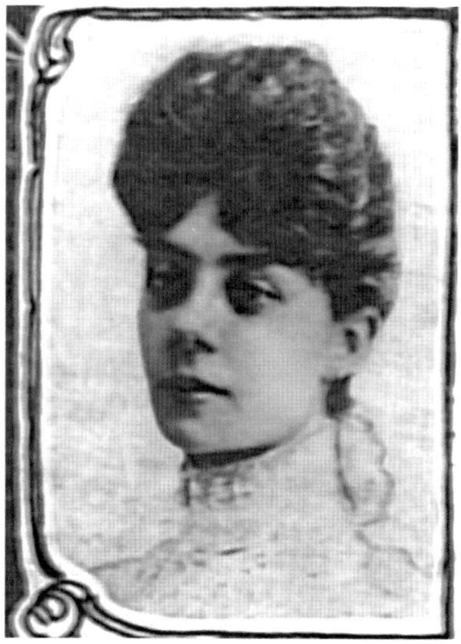

Iva Kistler's photo as it appeared in several newspapers the day following the accident. *Public domain.*

Dr. W. Todd Largent, who had offices over Dick Allen's menswear store on the east side of the square, was standing on the sidewalk below his office when the trouble began.

Patrons inside the Cheeves store included Leslie Bush, a prominent man from nearby Allen, Texas; about a dozen women; and two four-year-old children. Fannie Graves and her thirty-year-old daughter, Iva Kistler, were standing at the silk counter near the front of the store with Ira's four-year-old daughter, Anna.

Also positioned in the front of the store was customer Cassie Seay, a single woman of thirty-one. Cassie was a woman of refinement who was often mentioned in the society section of the local newspaper. Her parents died when she was a child, but the family of John Church, a local attorney and former county judge, had taken Cassie in as a foster daughter and raised her as their own. Cassie was worldly, college-educated and well traveled. She had lived in Dallas for four years, working as a secretary to the president of St. Mary's College. In 1909, she traveled to Oregon, Washington and California, remaining in California with relatives for several months and visiting the Hawaiian Islands. She returned to the Church home in McKinney in 1911 and was still living there in 1913.

Employees in the Cheeves store that day included a black porter who was reportedly not injured but never identified by name. Cheeves clerk Annie Curts was standing at the front of the store, behind a sales counter near the east wall. Annie and her associates Eva Searcy and Belle McWilliams were still recovering from the morning rush. Eva's sister, cashier Lula Searcy, was in the office. John Waller Thomas, the manager of the dress goods department, was wrapping a length of lace he had just cut for a customer. Another male clerk, Vernie Graves, was showing shoes to Lyda Moreland and Jennie Barnett at the back of the store. Norman Presley was ascending the stairs with a distinguished male customer, Leslie Bush. Luther Stephenson, the store's young delivery boy, had just returned to the store. He came through the back door and was headed to the office in the center of the store when he heard the building release a muffled moan.

The testimony of eyewitnesses varied somewhat when they were interviewed in the days following the calamity. Some claimed that one particular wall—or another—was the first to show signs of strain. There was little else to add—or was there? A trial several years later rekindled interest in the subject.

Most witnesses agreed that a groaning or grinding sound, accompanied by a slight swaying and bulging of the walls, lasted only seconds before the entire corner of the square seemed to tumble into the street, shattering and splintering objects indiscriminately. The fall gave rise to a plume of dense gray dust that rolled across the square like fog, obscuring vision and choking bystanders. In astonishment, the onlookers tried to process what they had just witnessed. What they remembered most clearly was the profound shock that overtook them—and the sense of panic that followed.

# 6
# BRICKS AND MORTAR

At 3:40 p.m., Annie Curts looked up in relief to see that the throng of customers continued to thin. The staff of nine employees working that day—four men and five women—had been scurrying around without a break. The shoppers had been drawn in by a well-advertised sale of ladies' intimates, merchandise kept near the store's entrance. This sale on undergarments naturally brought in a disproportionate number of female customers seeking assistance from female clerks. Seventy-two-year-old Ben Estes, a longtime employee and veteran of the original Mississippi Store, had been working that day, but just moments before 3:40 p.m., he left for the day. Estes's close brush with the disaster was so significant that the event was mentioned in his obituary when he died seven years later.

As Annie looked around, she noted that all the clerks within her range of sight were still engaged with customers. Her survey of the room amounted to a quick glance at the clock and a check on shoppers, but she picked up something odd and unsettling in the process.[58] With a feeling she later characterized as intuition, she focused for a second on the front of the store.[59] The wall seemed to bulge slightly, and a menacing noise, like a muffled chorus of squeaks, set off an alarm in her mind. As quickly as her body could react to the signal of danger, Annie dove to the floor behind the counter, covering her head. In an instant, the walls and floors above came crashing down around her with a thunderous roar she later compared to the sound of a cyclone.

Two young customers, Bessie Wade and Rosa Welch, had barely made it into the store when the crash occurred. Customer Thomas "Al" Bomar was standing in the doorway and looking into the Cheeves store when the first sign of trouble began. Bomar claimed that he saw the west side of the wall "heave to."[60] Bomar may have been holding the door for Bessie and Rosa as they came in or for Stella Russell and her nephew, who had just gone out. Acting on instinct, he darted into the street, sustaining a minor injury to his head caused by a fragment of brittle brick. Dr. Jonas Knight, who was standing near the building, scrambled out of the way of falling objects that seemed to explode behind him, spilling into the street in front of the store and to the east side of the buildings.

Also among those fortunate enough to make a quick exit was Luther Stephenson, the adolescent delivery boy who had entered the store through the back door just moments before the fall. He was positioned near the center of the store on the west side of the office when he detected an odd noise. Luther described the sound as a cracking noise and stated further that he believed it came from the direction of the partition wall that separated the Cheeves and Tingle stores. His reaction was immediate when he realized that the wall was buckling, and he reversed his course. With the advantage of his youth, Luther was nimble and his reflexes quick. He later explained that he feared opening the back door more than he feared breaking a window and escaping through its jagged panes.[61] His instincts served him well. He bolted through a window on the east side in the rear portion of the building and scurried to safety unharmed, emerging on the street on the east side, beyond the danger zone. Luther heard screams behind him but said he could see almost nothing due to the falling debris. Lula Searcy, who had been inside the office when Luther came in, was just steps behind him as he made his escape. The fact that she did not fare as well as he demonstrates how critical every second was to those attempting to escape.

Within seconds, splintered fragments of the two structures and their contents settled into a mountain of debris that one newspaper later described as standing thirty-five feet tall at its highest point. The rumble and vibration were thunderous, followed by an eerie silence. Within the rubble, twenty bodies, some of them lifeless, were ensnared, but stunned onlookers had little means of gauging that number.

In response to the sound, heard many blocks away, people descended on the square from every direction. From his newspaper office nearby, Walter Wilson heard the crash and was among the first to arrive on the scene. With little regard for their own safety, men began pulling away pieces of the jagged wreckage, and Wilson joined them. Rescuers may have silently speculated about the slim chances any human had for surviving such a bombardment, but they didn't allow skepticism to temper their efforts. Among them was Jim Thomas, who sustained a rather serious injury to his right hand while clawing through the rubble. His efforts were fueled by adrenaline and a desperate hope that he would find his brother John alive. Emotions also ran high among many members of the growing crowd of spectators. Because they could only guess at the number and identities of those inside, every friend and relative temporarily unaccounted for was thought to be a victim.

Hugh Kistler, co-owner of Kistler & Bristol's grocery store, was at work in his store on the east side of the square when he heard the accident. Kistler had no need to speculate; he knew for certain that his wife, Iva; the couple's four-year-old daughter, Anna; and his mother-in-law, Fannie Graves, had gone into the Cheeves stores shortly before the building collapsed. The trio had stopped in to see him just moments before and told him they were going to Cheeves. Kistler was overcome with fear and grief and initially collapsed under the strain. After struggling to maintain his composure, Kistler finally steadied himself and joined the rescue efforts.

William Morton "Mort" Shirley, who was working in his office in the courthouse building, soon learned that his wife—also named Iva—was among the victims. Mort was a man of many talents, serving as county treasurer in 1913 and also working as an insurance agent. He was a civil engineer, a graduate of Texas A&M, and had also studied law. Mort had once worked in banking, had been the county surveyor and had also been elected county clerk, serving two terms. In 1899, he sustained a serious injury when he was the victim of a train accident that left him with permanent complications and a weakened condition. In June 1911, he suffered a stroke that left him paralyzed from the waist down and doomed him to a "rolling chair" for the remainder of his life. Although challenged by his compromised health and a slew of medical bills, Mort Shirley remained cheerful and diligent in his work, earning the trust, respect and affection of everyone who knew him.

In 1913, Mort and Iva had two children, Gladys, fourteen, and Jack, five. Iva Shirley had been shopping at the Matthews Brothers store shortly before she decided to go to Cheeves. Jack had been with his mother that day, but fortunately, a friend at the Matthews store agreed to watch him while Iva made a quick trip to Cheeves. It might have been the elevator in the Matthews store that prompted young Jack to stay with the family friend, a decision that may have saved his life. After the accident, Mort Shirley stayed in his office with his young son and waited for news about his wife and the other victims, likely to spare Jack any additional trauma. As he sat and waited for word about his wife, Mort Shirley's own fear must have been overwhelming.

Stella Russell, a customer and resident of Farmersville who had just left the store with her young nephew Russell Hight when the fall occurred, was walking on the sidewalk in front of the store. She was thrown to the ground by the force of falling objects, her body covered with the sturdy fabric of an awning. She was fortunate that a large iron safe that fell from the third floor had missed landing on her. Rescuers, at first unaware that she was nearby, were attempting to move the safe when she stirred and cried out for help. Even as she was being rescued, she pleaded with workers to find her nephew. Walter Wilson was among those credited with freeing Stella; he later reported that her rescue had been the first.

In the earliest moments, the scene was chaotic, making it difficult for responders to distinguish escapees like Luther Stephenson and others from witnesses. People on the scene described a pair of lady customers who had escaped unharmed from positions near the front of the store. The two, who were quickly united with family members and whisked away, never publically identified themselves. Newspaper reporters from other towns, arriving on the scene long after the fall, were forced to get much of their information from secondhand sources. Among the sketchy items they printed was a vague reference to a black porter who escaped from inside the Cheeves store unharmed. The story, probably true, was never confirmed, nor was the story about the two ladies who vanished from the scene so quickly. These items were largely inconsequential, except that they confused efforts to make an exact accounting of the number of victims.

Amid the confusion and bedlam, Joe the Tamale Man, who was perhaps McKinney's best-known sidewalk vendor, reappeared in search of his cart of tamales. Rescue workers, frantic and in no mood to offer him sympathy or assistance, ordered the old man away.

Included in the mix of store occupants who escaped unscathed were the four adults and one child who were located in the Tingle store at the time of the fall. Tingle later claimed that he heard three loud cracks before the building came down, sounds he likened to cracking wallpaper. He and the others, in positions near the front door, were fortunate that the bulk of his store's considerable weight fell eastward rather than forward. One of the unfortunate reporting errors made by newspapers was a claim that both stores had been crowded with shoppers. As it related to Cheeves, the report was simply exaggerated with the use of this phrase: "men, women, and children thronged its counters."[62] There was a single customer in the Tingle store at the time of the accident.

Cheeves salesman Vernie Graves, who had been in the shoe department in the rear of the store when the buildings fell, was among the lucky. Graves survived the impact of falling debris and found his way to safety quickly and without the assistance of rescuers, as outlined in newspapers the following day. As the glut of materials, merchandise and store fixtures rained down, Graves was thrown to the floor by the weight of objects falling across his back. He soon gained his bearings and assessed his situation amid the foul air and unstable surroundings. The random positioning of falling objects had worked in his favor, producing a pocket of protection that insulated him and placed an intact ventilator shaft just above him. Even though the chute was narrow, reportedly two and a half feet in diameter, the force of falling objects thrust him through the shaft, landing him safely on the street.[63] It was quite a story—but was it true?

The *Weekly Democrat-Gazette* published this odd and dramatic account of Graves's escape, citing the *Fort Worth Record* as its source. A dozen other papers, including the *Fort Worth Star Telegram*, reported that Graves had simply escaped through a back window. The *Telegram* directly attributed the information to Graves, who had given an interview to a reporter. Whatever the truth about his escape, the result was the same: Vernie Graves escaped uninjured and was making the rounds, talking to reporters. Several papers quoted him, including one that stated that Graves had assured them that fifty people were in the Cheeves store at the time of the fall (almost double the actual number).[64]

Years later, when Lula Searcy testified in court about her experience that day, she stated under oath that she had seen Vernie Graves jump through a window on the east side of the of the building. Graves was likely just ahead of, or just behind, Luther Stevenson in hurling through that space. Since Lula had been able to see him, he had escaped before much of the building came down, obscuring vision and blocking out the light.

Vernie Graves had been assisting Jennie Barnett and Lyda Moreland shortly before the crash. All three were located in the shoe department in the back of the store, where victims seemed to have fared best. The reason for this was obvious by the light of the following day. The back portions of both stores were still standing, as were large sections of flooring on the rear portion of the upper floors, which had offered a degree of buffering to those below. Luther Stephenson's account of events also bore this out. He said, "I ran to the rear of the building and managed to get beyond the falling part of the structure."[65] Walter Wilson helped rescue Jennie Barnett and Lyda Moreland after he and others entered the collapsed structure from the rear. Barnett was largely unscathed, and Moreland was fortunate to walk away after her liberators uncovered her beneath a light layer of rubble. It seems that little was known about Barnett and Moreland; at least, little was written about the two after the accident. They may have been cousins. Virginia Tennessee "Jennie" Barnett was a young widow with two children; her maiden name was Moreland. Her husband, Lafayette Barnett, died in 1902, when he was just twenty-seven, leaving her with two young children.

Witnesses and victims later praised the determination of all rescuers, particularly the efficient leadership of Chief John McKinney. From his position in the McKinney Dry Goods store, he heard the fall and saw the creeping cloud of dust rolling across the street toward him. He summoned his volunteer firemen—a task he later said "was scarcely necessary"—then darted to the scene to direct rescue efforts.[66]

The quick-thinking chief sent foot messengers to direct storekeepers to close their shops, with the exception of those that might provide services to the rescue party. He asked that capable men stand by so that the groups could work in shifts, and requested that all available doctors be summoned. He requisitioned wagons, insisting that all items pulled from the wreckage be sorted into two categories: salvageable items, such as store inventory, and the battered remnants of building materials. Redeemable items were quickly and indiscriminately loaded onto waiting wagons and hauled away for sorting in other locations. Bricks, wood and steel beams were thrown into a large pile near the scene. The McKinney Dry Goods store furnished work gloves to rescue workers and fabric for shrouds. Workers were instructed to shout warnings before heaving objects on the pile of debris so that the pathway was clear. Injuries to rescuers were fairly common but none serious. Pickaxes and jackscrews—a type of nonmechanical lift that is operated by turning a large leadscrew—were among the few tools at the men's disposal. Throughout the ordeal, the chief rotated workers, insisting that a contingent of men withdraw when the numbers became too large to be efficient. Under the chief's leadership, and despite the absence of machinery, the progress was superhuman.

Within the first hour, volunteers realized that obstacles to their success were mounting. They began to see small flames leaping from beneath the rubble and realized that the early darkness of winter would soon be closing in. A crew of electricians hoisted a row of lights above the scene while workers continued to dig. The firemen intermittently doused the smoldering rubble with all the caution their heavy fire hoses would allow. Hot debris became heavy, slippery and laden with soot, and a layer of steam emanated from the heap.

Only a few yards, or perhaps *feet*, from the work of the busy pickaxes, were wounded victims beginning to stir within their darkened prison. They were trapped in blackness, some gasping to breathe, disoriented and, of course, terrified. But as is the human spirit, those who were able to do so began to communicate and move about, trying to evaluate their situation and hoping to survive long enough for rescuers to reach them. For the first twenty minutes or so, they did not realize that a small flame from an overturned stove had been released and was slowly spreading. Once they were aware of that fact, some realized that staying in place until rescuers arrived was no longer a good option.

## 7

# IS THAT YOU, MR. THOMAS?

While a swirl of activity was taking place outside the wreckage, several of the people trapped within recovered from the initial shock and confronted a horrifying reality. They were trapped, each likely imagining that he or she was the sole survivor. In reality, several people had survived the fall and were in various stages of injury and peril. Some were completely immobile, while others were free to move about within their individual confines but unable to assess their options and limitations due to the darkness. The survivors later said that they could not hear the rescue workers, at least not for a long while, but never doubted that their families and neighbors were searching for them. Some feared moving, lest they cause an avalanche, while others feared staying in place and suffocating more than the prospect of disturbing their precarious surroundings.

Most of the living owed their lives to the arbitrary—and in this case, fortunate—course that the falling objects had taken. Many had quite miraculously been spared a lethal pelting due to that phenomenon and sheer luck. In some cases, large, intact sections of ceiling and flooring came to rest at odd angles, creating protective triangular tents that absorbed the brunt of the impact for those lucky enough to be under them.

Within a few minutes of the fall, those able to communicate began doing so. The first victims to make contact were clerks Annie Curts and John Thomas, both positioned near the front of the store on the west side—neither critically injured. In both cases, it was specifically a large display counter that had provided lifesaving cover. Thomas struggled to gauge his situation, the debris around him so dense that he could barely move without dislodging objects. He could not see or hear the shouts of the rescue workers trying to reach him.

Although he had been stunned by the collapse, John Thomas had a sound memory of the moments immediately before and after the crash. He had been cutting and wrapping a piece of lace for a customer when small particles of ceiling plaster, "like sand," began to sift down and settle on the counter in front of him. He had just seen his associate, Norman Presley, along with customer Leslie Bush, ascending the nearby staircase. In an instant, he realized what was happening and, while calling out a warning to others, dove to the floor behind the counter. Thomas later recalled the experience, including the moment after the fall when he took stock of his situation, saying, "All was darkness, and the stillness was appalling for a few seconds."[67]

Nearby, but unbeknownst to John Thomas, Annie Curts was also conscious and trying to orient herself in her dark surroundings. She also remembered earlier moments clearly, as she had taken refuge under a counter. Like Thomas, the split-second decision almost certainly saved her life. The wall behind her collapsed onto the front of the counter where she had taken quick shelter. Afraid to stay where she was and hoping to find her way out, Annie groped around until she located a passageway free of debris. She inched through the crude and hazardous pathway until her probing fingers felt the unmistakable shape of a man's shoe. "Is that you Mr. Thomas?" she timidly asked.[68]

"I felt instinctively that it was John Thomas, who had been on the same side of the building as myself," she later told a reporter with the *Fort Worth Record*. "I was astonished at the calm manner in which I spoke. He answered in the affirmative, and then I asked him if he thought that we would get out alive." Thomas was kind but offered no false hope. "It looks like a slim change, Miss Annie," he replied. "And there we waited," said Annie.[69]

The pair of clerks did not wait long before they heard the voice of another survivor calling out to them. A customer, whose name John Thomas did not know, heard him speaking and called out from her location in one of the store's front showcase windows.[70] The customer had been pushed by the impact, landing in one of the store's large display windows, where she was immobilized. She called to Thomas, asking that he help her free herself because she could see a tiny ray of light near the center of the store and was determined to follow it. Thomas pleaded with her to remain still lest she dislodge other heavy objects, but the woman, who rested her hope on that tiny beacon of light, continued to work until she finally freed herself. Just as she had planned, she began crawling toward the light. Once there, the customer was convinced that a single timber was the only obstacle between death and safety, and she again pleaded with Thomas to help, asking that he come and remove the beam.

After giving into much prodding on the part of the customer, John Thomas agreed to help her. He could not see the ray of light but slowly and carefully crawled toward the sound of the woman's voice, with Annie following behind him. Annie, likely suffering from shock, pleaded with Thomas not to leave her. To the disappointment of all three, the beam was too massive and too heavily imbedded for Thomas to budge.

The three victims were there only a few minutes when they discovered that they had made a critical mistake in moving toward the center of the store. An overturned stove, situated near the office, had leaked its fuel and flame into the mix of rubble. The fire was beginning to find and feed on anything flammable within its grasp. The lady customer, in a desperate but feeble attempt to choke the flames, began lobbing fragments of glass toward them. The flames were terrifying, producing a low level of light that was clouded by smoke. The trio knew they would have to retrace their earlier steps to escape the growing heat. As the three made their way back to the front of the store, John Thomas heard, for the first time, the telltale, muffled voices of rescuers.

As they edged back to the front of the building, Belle McWilliams, a clerk who was trapped nearby, heard the voices of Thomas, Curts and the customer, and she called out to them. She was pinned and unable to move, she told them, and feared she would be burned to death. She pleaded with Thomas to rescue her, and although he tried to get to her, he could not get through the heavy debris that separated them. His inability to help her troubled him greatly, and he told her so. As he moved closer to the front, Thomas also heard the tiny voice of four-year-old Anna Kistler, trapped with her mother in a place where he could not see her, repeatedly asking in a calm voice, "Why don't papa come and get us?"[71]

At first, the victims were overjoyed and optimistic at the sounds of the rescuers, and a great feeling of calm settled over them, but the feeling faded with each passing minute. As the moments ticked by, the voices seemed no nearer, but the fire was gaining in intensity, creating suffocating smoke and agonizing heat. As the fire grew, the light made it possible for John Thomas to see three other victims in the distance. He recognized customer Cassie Seay and called out to her. He later said that he believed the other women were Eva Searcy and Iva Shirley, one of whom was bleeding profusely from a head wound.

In the days following the accident, Cassie Seay confirmed that she had been with Iva Shirley, but the third woman near them was Mary Emerson Stiff. Cassie and Iva were huddled near Mary, who was crushed so badly that she did not survive. In view of Mary's injuries, Seay considered her survival, and that of Iva Shirley, miraculous. She later explained that they owed their lives to the way one of the store's mammoth front doors came to rest. The door had fallen sideways, landing against a counter that propped up one end, protecting the space where the two were crouched. Mary, standing just a few feet away, had not been so fortunate.[72]

John Thomas positioned himself directly below the sounds of the pickaxes and voices. A large section of metal ceiling obstructed his view of the rescuers above and their view of him, but Thomas knew that the sound was a lifeline. He was determined to make enough noise to ensure that those outside heard him. Seeing that a large piece of metal was firmly lodged and was holding back a mountain of wreckage overhead, he did not attempt to move it but began knocking on the metal. Intermittently, he knocked and shouted forcefully until he became too hoarse and weak to continue. On the other side of that metal plate, workers finally heard him, but they were also finding it impossible to jar the metal piece. In desperation, they engaged a saw.

As the victims waited, the heat became so stifling that Annie lost consciousness—her last words, "I am burning up, oh, I am burning up."[73] John Thomas knew that their only chance for survival rested with the sawing that seemed far too slow to save them. He later said that rescuers had saved him from a "burning death." Indeed they had. The slow but steady sawing finally rewarded the men's efforts.

Once rescuers pulled away the last impediments to freedom, Thomas lifted the customer, and then Annie, through the crude opening. As anxious as he was to breathe fresh air, he was forced to take a minute to gather his strength before he was able to lift himself up to a point where his liberators could pull him to safety. For those who had suffered through it, the ordeal seemed interminable. In reality, the trio of survivors had been trapped for slightly less than an hour.

Within minutes, rescuers opened a second opening nearby from which they quickly freed Iva Shirley, then Cassie Seay. Cassie was taken to the McKinney Dry Goods store across the street for evaluation. Once she was pronounced uninjured, she called her foster mother, Julia Church, to let her know she was safe. Injured both physically and psychologically, Annie Curts was taken to one of McKinney's four privately owned hospitals. Her last memory inside the dungeon of debris was of breaking a glass case so that she could thrust her hands inside in search of cooler air. John Thomas was taken to a nearby hotel for an assessment. As he was being carried away, he told rescuers where they could find Belle McWilliams, hoping it was not too late. Stella Thomas, John's wife, had been working to prepare for a banquet at the First Christian Church when the buildings fell. She rushed to the scene in such haste, one newspaper reported, that she had done so bareheaded. It is an interesting point, suggesting that proper ladies were expected to wear hats when they went out in public, almost without exception. John Thomas first believed that he was only bruised but later learned the full extent of his injuries. He had received many blows to his hands, head and limbs and was suffering from exhaustion and exposure to intense heat and smoke.

Belle McWilliams, the clerk John Thomas had been forced to abandon, was finally freed from the heavy lumber that had restricted her movement. It took saws and heavy lifting to dislodge the timber that pinned her back and legs, proof that John Thomas could not have saved her by himself. The fifty-three-year-old mother of three was sent to a hospital with injuries that were pronounced life-threatening, but she eventually made a full recovery.

Hugh Kistler's efforts to find his wife, daughter and mother-in-law were rewarded when he and other workers freed Iva Kistler and little Anna. Witnesses said that Hugh Kistler covered his daughter with kisses. Iva Kistler and Fannie Graves, mother and grandmother to Anna, had tried to shield the child when they sensed danger, throwing themselves over her small frame. The attempt was successful to a large degree, the child suffering nothing serious, except perhaps a broken finger. Iva and Fannie fared worse, but all three survived the ordeal.

Because the buildings had primarily collapsed eastward, sparing the back walls, there was a point of entry at the rear of the store that Dr. Jonas Knight and others used to locate victims. Knight located clerk Lula Searcy, who was pinned under a heavy beam. Lula had been in the office when the first hint of trouble began and was attempting to follow Luther Stevenson to safety when she was struck down under the weight of falling objects. She was alert when found and communicated with Dr. Knight and others as they worked to free her. It took the efforts of the good doctor and several others to delicately raise the heavy piece of wood that held her. Dr. Knight sustained a rather serious back injury from the heavy lift, but the group was successful in freeing Searcy. Lula's younger sister Eva, on the opposite side of the store, was unaccounted for.

Walter Wilson, co-owner of the *Democrat*, likely never witnessed a story more relevant to his community, yet he worked the emergency alongside his neighbors. Ever the prudent newsman and historian, he understood the value that pictures of the fast-changing scene would soon have and acted on that instinct. He managed to rouse a photographer, Hal Greenwood, owner of the Blue Gallery photography studio on South Tennessee Street, who brought his camera to the site, climbed to an upper window in the courthouse and captured several disquieting images.[74] After helping to free Stella Russell and arrange for photographs, Wilson rushed back to his print shop, where he began sending wires to other, larger newspapers, a task he continued until midnight.

In retrospect, it seems that nothing short of a miracle made it possible for workers to pull so many from the ghastly mountain of ruins so quickly. But sadly, heroics, determination and a seemingly endless supply of helpers simply could not produce a happy ending for everyone.

# 8
# A BLANKET OF SORROW

Among the first fatalities discovered was Mary Emerson Stiff, age twenty-seven, whose battered and crushed body was brought out and taken to McKinney's only undertaker, Crouch-Hartzog.[75] She was pinned beneath a large wooden beam and, although rescued alive, died shortly after being moved. Although she was an adult and the mother of two, Mary lived with her widowed mother. With Mary's death, her mother, who was also named Mary, was forced to bury her fourth child, and she became the guardian of Mary's two young sons, Thomas, seven, and Edwin, five. Although the young boys were left without a mother, they were fortunate in at least one respect. Their mother was a savvy businesswoman who left them financially secure. Mary owned several pieces of rental property and had insured her life for $2,000, naming her sons as beneficiaries. A court-appointed administrator managed the money until the boys were of legal age and paid their grandmother a monthly allowance to cover their expenses. Mary Emerson Stiff was buried in McKinney's Pecan Grove Cemetery beside her beloved brother Mack, who had died in 1902 at age twenty-three.[76]

Eva Searcy, a clerk and younger sister of another Cheeves employee, Lula Searcy, did not survive her injuries. Eva, twenty-five, only lived about twenty minutes after being taken out. Eva and Lula were two of seven siblings in a family devastated by the loss of young Eva. The Searcy family placed a message of gratitude in the local newspaper, thanking friends for the abundance of support and many floral arrangements they had received.

The last line of their haunting note reflected the depth of their gratitude and sorrow: "May your lives be as sweet and beautiful as the flowery bed under which our Eva now so peacefully rests." Among Eva's pallbearers were co-workers John Thomas and Vernie Graves.

Three young female Cheeves customers, all of whom suffered a fatal pummeling that likely caused immediate death, were taken to the Crouch-Hartzog mortuary. Dr. J. Eber Hunter issued their death certificates, entering this cause of death on each document: "collapsed building, sudden death."[77] The three had barely embarked on adulthood. Kate Milligan turned nineteen just weeks before her death; Rosa Welch was thirty-one, and Bessie Wade was twenty-two.

Kate Milligan, born on December 3, 1893, in McKinney, was one of four children born to Robert Jackson "Jack" Milligan and his wife, Lydia. Jack was a farmer and also worked at a local mill. Kate's family also expressed thanks to friends by placing a note in the local newspaper, referring to Kate as the rose of the family and assuring friends that the support they offered had helped them bear their sorrow.[78]

Rosa Lee Welch was born in 1882 and was the only daughter (apart from a sister who died at age two) in a family with three boys. Her father, John T. Welch, was widowed in 1908, when Rosa's mother, Mollie, died after a lingering sickness. Rosa had taken care of her mother throughout the ordeal.[79]

The death certificate for Bessie Wade, a telephone operator, was sparsely completed, there being no one present at the time of her death to supply much of the basic information. Her friend and shopping companion that day, Rosa Welch, had also perished. Bessie had only lived in McKinney for a year and was engaged to wed at the time of her death.[80] She was seventy-six miles from family members, who still lived in Yantis, Wood County, where she had been raised. The *Weekly Democrat-Gazette* reported that Bessie worked for Southwestern Telephone Company. Another of Bessie's friends, Leona Southall, was working for the Union Telephone Company on the day of the accident, located in the building across the street from the Cheeves store. Leona was frantic to know of Bessie's fate but faithfully manned her post as one of several long-distance operators whose services were badly needed. J.A.S. Smith of Dallas, Bessie's stepbrother, arrived in McKinney on Friday morning to claim her body and make arrangements to return her remains to Yantis for burial.

The death of four-year-old Russell Hight was particularly tragic. He had gone to the Cheeves store that day in the company of his Aunt Stella, and

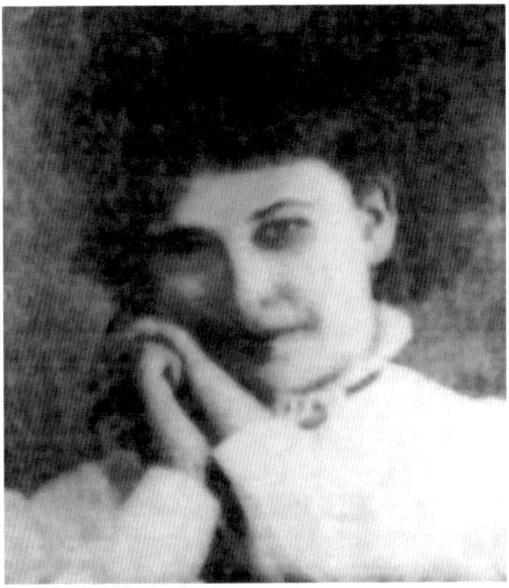

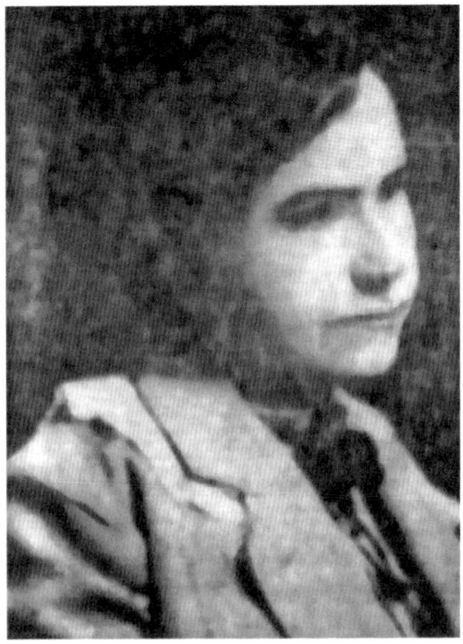

*Left*: Kate's picture as it appeared in several newspapers on the day following the accident. *Public domain.*

*Right*: Rosa's picture as it appeared in several newspapers on the day following the accident. *Public domain.*

the pair had just exited the building when falling objects separated the two. After Stella Russell was discovered under a felled awning, she was frantic and desperate to find the child. Rescuers found the little fellow, but the news was devastating: he had been crushed to death.

Russell Hight was a towheaded, angelic-looking child, the son of Robert "Leslie" Hight and Stella's sister Lelia. Robert was a realtor with the R.L. Land Company, his office located above the Collin County National Bank on the town square, just a few doors away from the collapsed buildings. The story was troubling enough on its surface, but those who knew the Hight family knew that they had lost another child, an eighteen-month-old daughter, to illness the previous May. Russell was buried in McKinney's Pecan Grove Cemetery next to his sister, Linnie Lucille. At the time of Russell's death, Robert and Lelia Hight had one other child, an infant son named Eugene. They later added a daughter to the family.

As rescue efforts continued in downtown McKinney, a tragedy of a different kind was unfolding in a residence on North Tucker Street. At approximately 5:30 p.m., Lura Perry, twenty-four, gave birth to a healthy baby boy in the home of her parents, Mr. and Mrs. Jonas D. Bass. Unfortunately, Lura

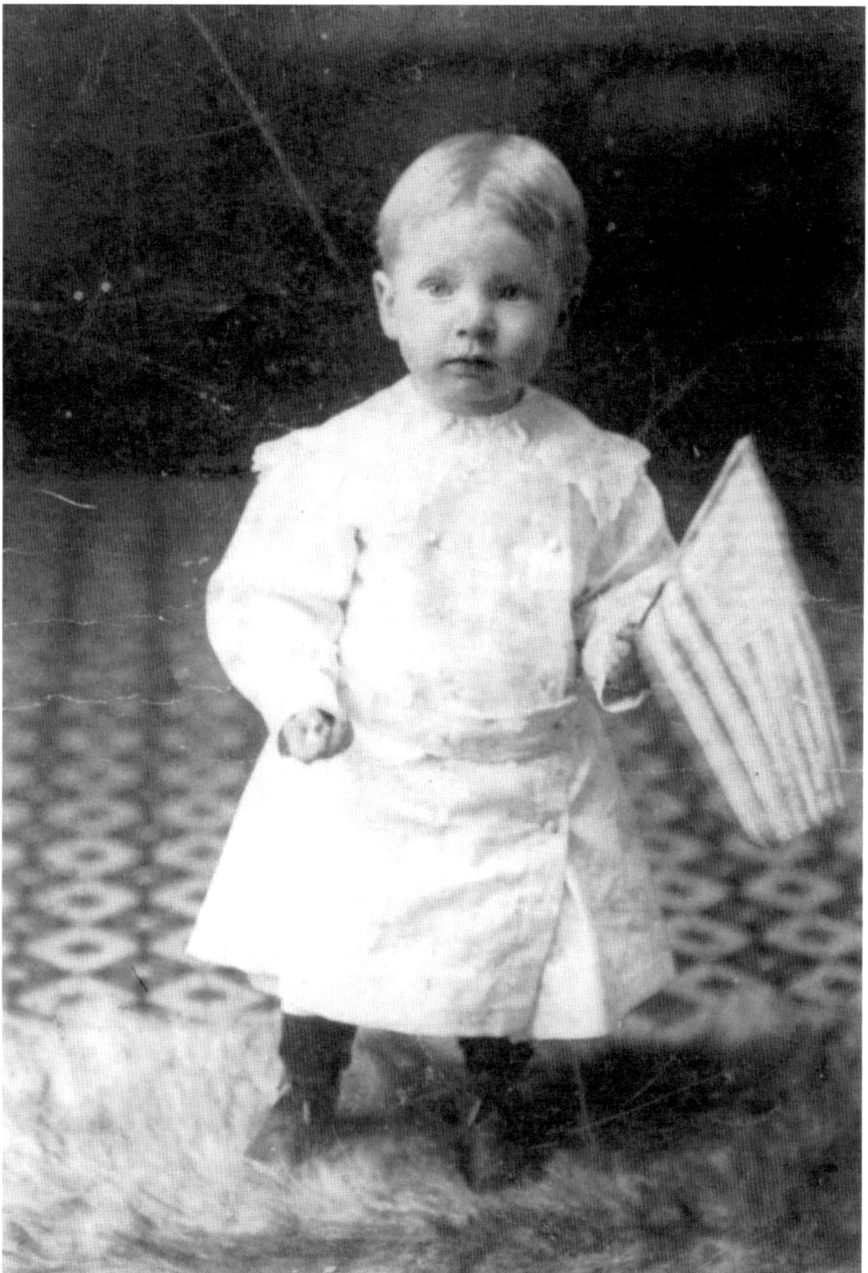

Russell Hight. *Courtesy of Martha Prince.*

experienced complications from the birth and required the attention of a doctor. Her anxious family tried to summon a physician, but due to the accident on the square, none could be found, and Lura died.

There was some irony attached to this sad story. Lura Perry actually lived in Fort Worth with her in-laws, Mr. and Mrs. Thomas C. Perry, but had gone to her childhood home in McKinney to have her baby. She and James Lynn Perry, a traveling salesman and former McKinney resident, had married on October 20, 1909. Lura's father-in-law, Thomas C. Perry, was a former resident of McKinney; in fact, he represented the "Perry" in Perry, Murphy and Company and was the co-founder of McKinney's original Mississippi Store.

Thomas Perry relayed this story to a newspaper: On the afternoon of the twenty-third, as he sat at a desk in the Worth Hotel waiting for news of the birth of his grandchild, he was writing a letter to his brother-in-law and old business associate George Murphy, who still lived in Sherman. In his letter, Perry marveled about the news of the collapsed store he and Murphy had founded twenty-six years earlier. But before he finished the letter, Perry received the disturbing news that his daughter-in-law had died from the complications of childbirth.[81]

The baby was a healthy boy; his name, as entered on his birth certificate, was Thomas Lynn Perry. Lura's parents raised the child, who apparently later changed his name to Lynn Bass Perry. Many people speculated that Lura Perry might have survived with the assistance of a doctor's care that January evening. Dr. J. Eber Hunter, who signed at least four of the death certificates for those killed in the collapse, also signed the birth certificate for newborn Thomas Lynn Perry.

Some speculators later theorized that the commotion and weight of the great crowd that had patronized Cheeves on the day of the collapse had somehow caused the fall. However, not a single witness located inside the store disputed the fact that all of the customers and employees in the Cheeves store were confined to the lower floor at the time of the fall, with two exceptions. Customer Leslie Bush had requested assistance from John Thomas just moments before the crash, but Thomas was busy with another customer. Salesman Norman Presley stepped forward to assist Bush, and the two men began climbing the stairs.

The battered remains of sixty-two-year-old Leslie Walker Bush—the last body taken out of the smoldering ruins—were removed about 9:30 p.m. The location of his body, found on the store's east sidewalk beneath a mountain of debris, was proof that he had absorbed the full force of the collapsing third floor, his body propelled by (and with) falling wreckage and covered under many layers. His death was believed to have been instantaneous and recorded as such on his death certificate by Dr. Hunter. Leslie's brother Walter, the president of the First National Bank of Greenville, identified the body.

Leslie Bush's descendants characterized him as a frugal yet generous man, a gentle soul who adored his favorite horse and buggy and loathed Johnson grass. Bush was a prominent man who owned much real estate, including a sprawling farm and ranch near Allen, where he had lived since 1884. He had many personal and business connections to McKinney and was a member of one of Collin County's pioneer families. He was a proponent of education, eager to obtain good schooling for his six children and generous in support of other educational endeavors. Bush's son Walter was a cashier at the Continental State Bank in McKinney at the time of the elder Bush's death. Leslie Bush was the father of five grown, or nearly grown children and a twelve-year-old daughter, also named Leslie. His wife and children crafted an emotion-packed note of public thanks for publication in the newspaper, just as the Searcy and Milligan families had done.

Leslie Bush's will offers some insight into his personality. Coincidentally, it was prepared on January 18, 1913, less than a week before his death. Bush left specific instructions in his will that he be "buried in a decent and Christian-like manner," a request that was obviously important to him.[82] Bush owned a half interest, along with his brother, in about 1,500 acres in Collin and Brazoria Counties that the brothers had inherited from their father. In addition to his inherited property, Leslie Bush had acquired many acres of land on his own during his lifetime. He also owned cattle worth an estimated $1,000 at the time of his death and stock in two local banks and Allen's water company. The aggregate value of his stock was $6,300.

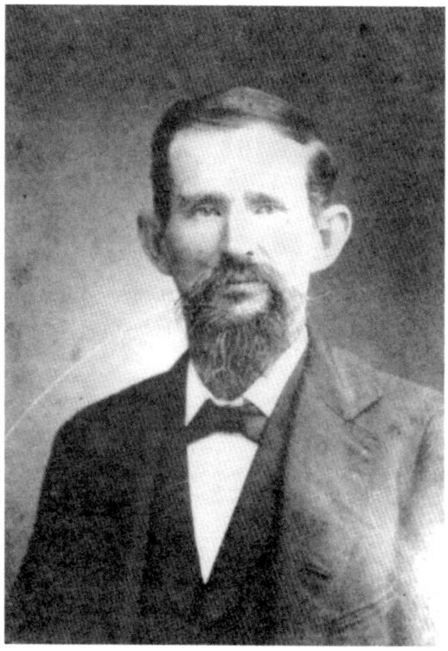

Leslie W. Bush. *Courtesy of Nancy Bush Morian.*

Bush's family and friends honored his request for a reverent funeral. Elder R.C. Horn, who kept a journal from 1871 to 1936, attended the funeral and noted the event. Horn wrote that a "large audience" attended the funeral at the Bush home and that he was among several ministers who offered prayers and biblical passages.[83]

The most haunting death was that of Norman Presley. Presley, age thirty-five, was a quiet man who had spent his adult life working in the retail business. Although he was raised in Bowie, Texas, he was well known in McKinney, because he had once managed the Nickel store in McKinney and later opened his own racket store. He and his wife, Sophia, were popular and the parents to a thirteen-month-old daughter named Emma Lou.

Without question, Norman Presley's story was the most tragic, because his suffering was immense. Presley had been going up the stairs with customer Leslie Bush at the time of the fall. He was pinned in the wreckage near the middle of the store, where he was inaccessible to rescuers and the fire was most intense. John Thomas and Annie Curts, from positions much farther away, had found the blistering heat and thick smoke unbearable, but Norman Presley was entirely without options. Firemen were able to speak to him and came close enough to him that they could offer Presley a bucket of water and sponge so that he could relieve his thirst. But try as they might, they could do little else to relieve his suffering from the blistering heat, the worst of which was concentrated on his feet. Rescuers marveled at Presley's courage and stamina. He complained little and begged them to locate and administer aid to Leslie Bush, his last customer. When the pain became unbearable, Presley's rescuers claimed that he begged for a gun to end his misery—a request none was willing to grant. Norman Presley was condemned to hours of agony. He was alive when released from his confines and taken out but died shortly after from ghastly burns.

Sophia Presley, who was in Dallas when she heard the news of the collapse, set out immediately for McKinney but found it difficult to make the trip because the interurban cars were overloaded. Norman died before she could reach him.

At 11:00 p.m., John McKinney gathered a few of his men and Mayor Henry Finch for a consultation. The men had done an exceptional job, clearing away enough debris that they agreed to call a halt to the rescue work for the night, and were relatively confident that no one, at least no one *living*, was still trapped therein. Their judgment proved sound; an assessment of the victims showed that eight dead and twelve injured had been pulled from the wreckage, all within a period of roughly six hours. That initial tally never changed.

The Cheeves brothers, much like Sophia Presley, found it difficult to reach McKinney quickly. Three of them, Thomas, Whitt and Patrick, eventually made it into town, where they drew up this message and placed it in the next addition of the local paper:

> *To the good people of McKinney and Collin County: We cannot command language to express our feelings over the great calamity that has befallen us in the recent destruction of our store. We cannot tell you our feelings, because we cannot take each one of you by the hand and express our true sentiments to you. Our financial loss is nothing—we do not grieve over this because we can replace this, and we only wish we could replace the precious lives that were taken so suddenly. This, and only this, is the one burden on our hearts. While we could not prevent the sad accident, yet we cannot but feel sad with the good people of McKinney in this bereavement. We want to thank the noble men who went to the rescue, and who worked so faithfully to save those who were caught in the building. To those who were so unfortunate to lose some dear one, we extend our deepest sympathy, and may God in His infinite goodness give you grace to bear this ordeal. We trust that those who were rescued will speedily recover. We are too sad over the loss of the lives to say more.* *Cheeves Bros. and Co.*[84]

The Cheeves brothers had an acute understanding of the pain the families were experiencing. In 1913, the Cheeves brothers numbered four—they had once numbered five. They had lost one of their own in another catastrophe involving a Cheeves store many years before, but the memory and the pain were still fresh.

# 9
# SMILE AND SAY CHEEVES

The Cheeves Brothers name was once familiar and esteemed in Central Texas, synonymous with sophistication and class in a crowed area of commerce—the dry goods business. During a time when local residents generally owned all of the local retail establishments in developing towns, the Cheeves brothers dared to insert themselves. The success of their stores, many of which operated for many decades, was proof that they fulfilled a need by offering amenities that were not generally available in small towns. The company's buyers, including some women, periodically traveled to markets in the Northeast to secure the latest in fashion, which they bought in volume. Creatively dressed store windows at all Cheeves stores showcased trends, tempting passersby. Second-level balconies, a feature found in finer stores, were popular with the brothers. Men's furnishings were a specialty at Cheeves stores, where suits bearing the Cheeves label were fitted with the care an artist applies to his craft.

Today, a building that once housed a Cheeves Brothers store in Temple, Texas, is home to an upscale steakhouse.[85] The owner thoughtfully restored the interior, saving its elegant, nostalgic features while cleverly capturing the Cheeves theme using an abstract emblem of a bowler hat and an impeccably manicured mustache.[86]

The Cheeves conglomerate was fluid, undergoing many changes over the years, but despite those changes, the astute brothers made sure that the shopping experiences of their patrons, and thus the Cheeves Brothers' reputation, were not compromised. While family members firmly held the reins of the business, several other men joined and left the Cheeves roster of investors and managers over the years.

There were five Cheeves brothers, but only three left a discernable imprint on the company that bore their name. The patriarch of this Cheeves family was Andrew Jackson Cheeves (1835–1918). Andrew and his wife, Nancy Herren Cheeves (1837–1918), were the parents of five sons and three daughters. Andrew, an Alabamian by birth, was a proud veteran of the Confederacy and a capable farmer. All of the couple's children were born in Alabama between 1855 and 1878 and raised on the Cheeves farm, where they learned the value of hard work. In order of birth year, those offspring were

1. Thomas Alexander Cheeves (1855–1918)
2. Mary Cheeves (Moore) (1857–1932)
3. Patrick E. Cheeves (1864–1918)
4. Stephen Whitfield "Whitt" Cheeves (1868–1930)
5. Rebecca Cheeves (Rogers) (1872–1944)
6. Evaline "Evie" Cheeves (Johnson) (1874–1953)
7. Samuel W. Cheeves (1876–1893)
8. Richard Denman Cheeves (1878–1944)

Although all of the family members eventually landed in Texas, they came at different times and settled in scattered locations around Central Texas. The eldest son, Thomas, and his sister Mary led the migration to Texas in the 1870s.[87] Thomas landed first in Waco then moved to Falls County, while Mary and her husband, Alexander Moore, settled on a farm in Bosque County, eventually raising a dozen children.

Once situated in Falls County, Thomas spent his time between the small communities of Reagan and Marlin, just nine miles apart. His decision to open a store in Reagan, and the decision of two of his brothers to move near him soon after, set a course for the future Cheeves Brothers enterprise. Patrick and Whitt moved to Reagan, where they assisted Thomas with his dry goods business. Thomas also partnered with a man named Lysias B. Chilton, operating a store in Marlin called Chilton and Cheeves. It appears that the business was successful, but after a few years, Chilton relinquished his share, selling it to Cheeves on September 23, 1890, for $22,276.23, the equivalent of over $500,000 today.[88] Chilton, who was only thirty-nine years old and the father of six, died only a month after separating from the business. In 1894, his widow, Ida, married a man named Bradley J.

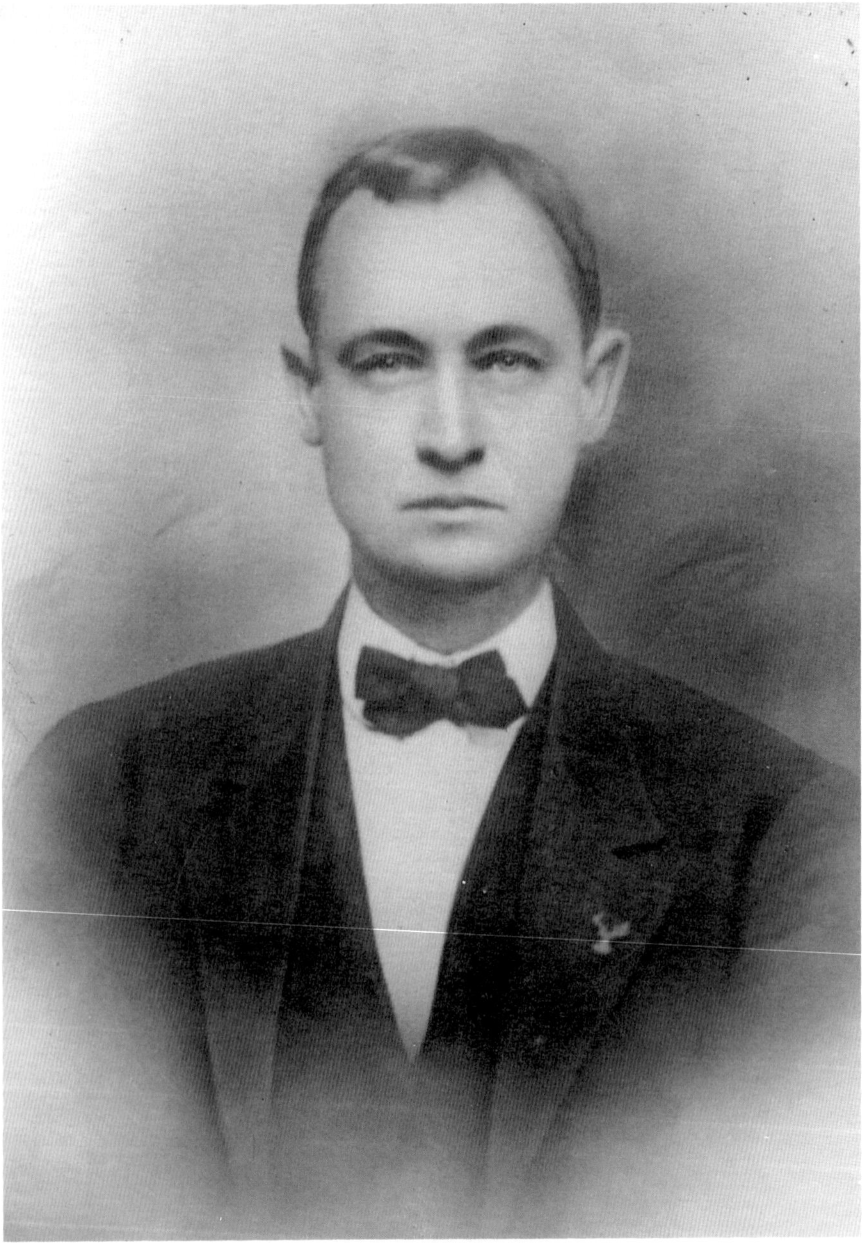

Patrick Cheeves. *Courtesy of Ferol Richardson and Ed Hinkle.*

Linthicum, who was, or soon became, the next Cheeves partner in Marlin. By 1897, stores bearing the Cheeves and Linthicum name were operating in Calvert, Taylor and Marlin.[89] Thomas moved to Marlin, and Whitt Cheeves moved to Calvert to manage that store. Whitt managed the Calvert store for some time before moving to Temple and finally to Cameron, where he lived for the rest of his life, overseeing all of the Cheeves stores.

On April 1, 1892, Thomas Cheeves opened a store in Temple, a town located in Bell County about thirty miles southwest of Marlin. Bradley Linthicum had no stake in the Temple store, but Patrick Cheeves did.[90] Patrick moved to Temple within a few months of the store opening, and he initially acted as an assistant to store manager J.M. Osbourne. But Patrick Cheeves, age twenty-nine, was not entirely well. In September 1893, a Temple newspaper reported that he had returned to work after an absence of several weeks due to a chronic illness.

Soon, young Samuel Cheeves, the fourth brother to do so, moved from Alabama to Texas to join the growing family business. He left behind his parents and younger brother Richard, the last of the family living in Alabama. Sam lived in Marlin, near Thomas, but worked wherever he was needed, often in Temple.

On the night of December 6, 1893, less than two years after it opened, tragedy struck at the Temple location. The accident caused the Cheeves family a loss of an estimated $35,000 worth of inventory and the life of their beloved Sam. The Temple store operated out of a one-story brick rental owned by a man named W.A. Wilkerson, located on Fourteenth Street at Avenue D.[91] The Cheeves store adjoined a small grocery store, Winkleman and Freeman. The grocery store was new, having opened only three months earlier.

Things had gone well at the Cheeves Temple store except for a rash of late-night, break-in robberies. Three of the store's young clerks, perhaps in an attempt to catch the burglars, slept on cots in the back room of the store. Just past midnight on the morning of December 7, 1893, a fire thought to have come from the remnants of trash burned in the alleyway earlier, began on the grocer's side of the building. The fire department answered the call but struggled to gain enough water pressure to extinguish the flames. They were unaware that the three young store clerks—Frank Rogers, Dan Boyles and Sam Cheeves—were sleeping in the back room of the Cheeves store. Miraculously, a bystander caught sight of two of the boys staggering about and helped them find their way to safety. Boyles and Rogers suffered from serious smoke inhalation but recovered. Sam Cheeves's lifeless body was found near the back door about 9:00 a.m., burned beyond recognition. He was seventeen years old.

Soon after the fire, the Temple store, which was covered by insurance, reopened at a location on Twelfth Street. In the years that followed, matters related to the Cheeves business and family occurred in rather quick succession. In 1896, Patrick supervised the establishment of new stores in Mexia, Limestone County, and Waxahachie, Ellis County. Two years later, on August 12, 1898, Cheeves's Temple store moved into a grand, three-story building on Avenue A. In its new and larger space, the Temple store added a large millinery department, furniture and even groceries to its inventory. In Marlin, Bradley Linthicum became a vice president (later president) of the First National Bank, divesting himself of his holdings in all Cheeves stores.

By the turn of the twentieth century, the migration of Cheeves family members from Alabama to Texas was complete. In 1900, brothers Patrick and Whitt—both of whom were married—lived in Temple. Sometime between 1900 and 1910, Whitt moved to Cameron in Milam County, but Patrick Cheeves remained in Temple for the rest of his life. Also, by 1900, the elder Cheeves, Andrew and Nancy, with their youngest son, Richard, had relocated to Texas, the last of the family to do so. They settled in Temple, in a modest home on Sixth Street that remained in the family for many years. Richard, who was twenty-two in 1900, and his father, Andrew, worked as salesmen in the Temple store. Sister Rebecca also made the move to Texas, marrying Frank C. Rogers in 1900 and making her home in Waxahachie, where Frank managed the Waxahachie store. Evaline Cheeves married Enoch C. "Clifton" Johnson and settled in Temple; Clifton joined the management staff of the Temple store in 1900. They lived near Andrew in a house near the store on Sixth Street; both Cheeves homes have since been torn down.

In its February 5, 1903 edition, the *Weekly Democrat-Gazette* of McKinney referred to the Cheeves Brothers enterprise as "one of the most extensive dry good firms in Texas" when it announced that Thomas Cheeves had purchased the Mississippi Store from William Purnell.[92] Initially, only two members of the Cheeves inner circle held stake in the new store: Thomas and Whitt Cheeves. The existence of another partner, a man named J.B.E. Brown, was short-lived.

The McKinney Cheeves store was well received and enjoyed good patronage. An article in McKinney's *Weekly Democrat-Gazette*, published on March 7, 1907, offered these glowing comments about the enterprise:

> *The firm of Cheeves Bros. & Co. is widely known throughout Collin County, and their reputation for fair dealing has built them up a trade second to none in the city. Mr. O.C. Stewart, who has been manager for the firm since their first advent into this city, is greatly responsible for their success....*[H]*e has, by close attention to the firm's business, attained a reputation as a* [good] *manager, which is certainly deserved. It is with pride that we point to the large dry goods firm of Cheeves Bros. & Co. as one of our leading business institutions.*

Over the years, Thomas, Whitt and Patrick made many investments in their respective hometowns, including local banks, where they were board members and/or officers. In 1909, Cheeves Bros and Company partnered with A.L. Flint of Temple in building a large commercial building on Second Street between Central Avenue and Avenue A. Thomas was an aggressive investor. Among other things, he held stake in local utilities, a small oil company, commercial property, a large hotel, a mineral water company and a bathhouse in Marlin.

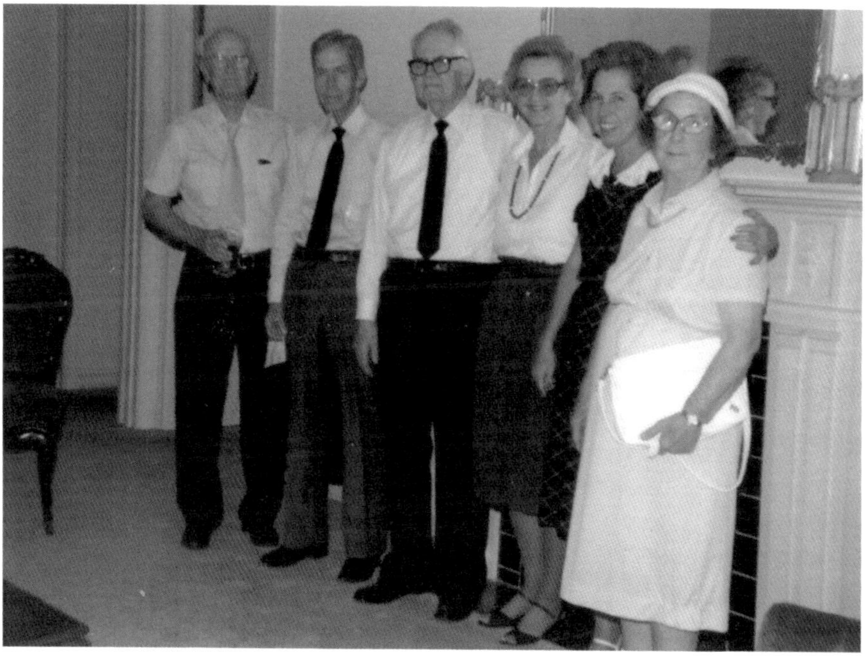

Second generation of Cheeves family members to those who owned and operated the original stores (*left to right*): Thomas A. Cheeves Jr., Enoch C. Johnson, Hubert Johnson, a family friend, Patsy Hinkle (granddaughter of Pat Cheeves) and Ferol Cheeves (widow of Pat Cheeves). Picture taken in 1971. *Courtesy of Ferol Richardson and Ed Hinkle.*

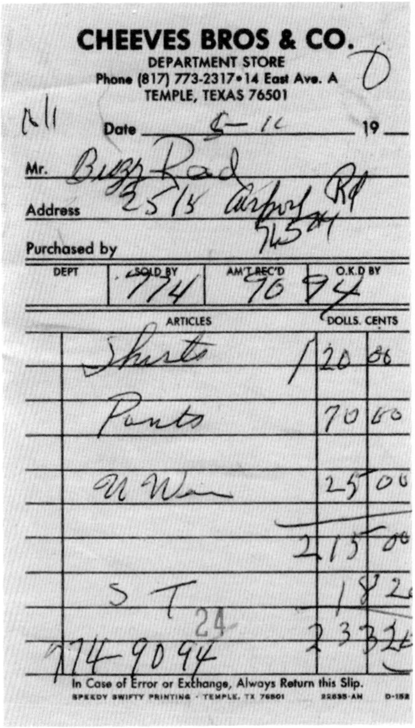

CHEEVES BROS & CO.
DEPARTMENT STORE
Phone (817) 773-2317 • 14 East Ave. A
TEMPLE, TEXAS 76501

Date ______ 19__

Mr. ______

Address 2518 Airport Rd

Purchased by

| DEPT | SOLD BY | AM'T REC'D | O.K.D BY |
|---|---|---|---|
| | 774 | 7094 | |

| ARTICLES | DOLLS. | CENTS |
|---|---|---|
| Shirts | 120 | 00 |
| Pants | 70 | 00 |
| | 25 | 00 |
| | 215 | 00 |
| S T | 18 | 2[illegible] |
| | 233 | 2[illegible] |

774-9094

In Case of Error or Exchange, Always Return this Slip.

SPEEDY SWIFTY PRINTING · TEMPLE, TX 76501

*Left*: A receipt from the Cheeves Brothers Temple store. *Courtesy of Ed Hinkle.*

*Below*: The building where the McKinney Cheeves store relocated after the accident, as it appears today. *Author's collection.*

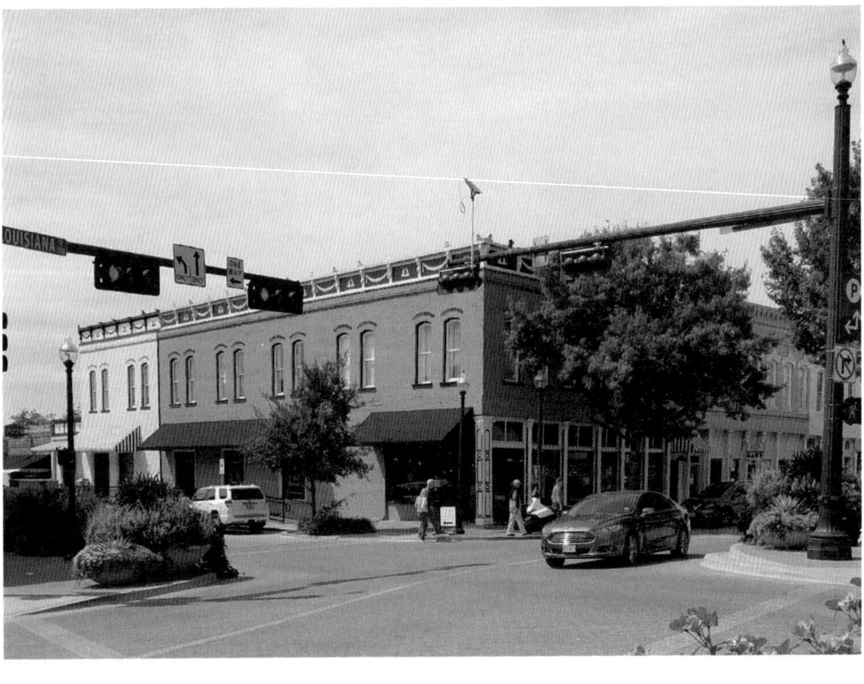

In 1912, Thomas completed work on a four-bedroom/four-bath, 6,635-square-foot mansion in Marlin. The Cheeves brothers were well known and respected, each a stalwart in his community and devoted family man. Richard "Dick," the youngest, never married. Dick worked in the Temple store for many years, but it appears that he was not involved with the other stores to a large degree. When he died in 1944, he was the last Cheeves brother to go, leaving only sister Evaline Johnson, who died in 1953. Evaline's two sons, Enoch "Clifton" Johnson and Hubert Johnson, took over management of the Temple store, where they worked for several decades.

After the McKinney store collapsed, three of the Cheeves brothers made their way to town as quickly as they could, offering a heartfelt public condolence in the newspaper. They understood the pain of losing a loved one. Even so, in the usual Cheeves fashion, they maintained their composure, made the necessary decisions and regained their commercial footing with remarkable speed. Within a week of the accident, the *Weekly Democrat-Gazette* announced that the community was pleased to learn that the Cheeves store would soon be reopening in a new location on the southwest corner of the square.

# 10
# HEROES AND VILLAINS

The days following the ordeal were ones of sorrow and reflection. Even amid the sadness, people found much to praise. The outpouring of help had been overwhelming, both from within the county and from outlying communities. Offers of help continued to pour in for several days. Mayor Finch and Chief McKinney were forced to decline many of the offers but were grateful for all. On the night of the accident, the City of Dallas had been poised to ship its engine-powered fire truck on a flatbed interurban car. The interurban had readied the flatbed before learning that John McKinney had declined the offer. A collective bid for help came from Dallas undertakers, who agreed to send men to relieve the strain on McKinney's only embalmer. After receiving a nod, the group sent six undertakers.

Assistance arrived in many forms. At the request of W.H. Bush, Leslie's brother, the Katy railroad arranged a special run on the evening of the accident, transporting passengers the forty-four-mile distance between Greenville and McKinney. The train was loaded with an estimated three hundred, including many reporters, nurses and doctors. The special train stayed in McKinney to accommodate the need for a late-night return to Greenville. Doctors who chose to ride the interurban to McKinney were given priority and free passage. Once in McKinney, volunteers found hot coffee available to them, compliments of a group of local women who wanted to show their appreciation.

On the afternoon of the accident, the Union Telephone Company, located upstairs in a building across the side street just east of Cheeves, had become a critical player in the area of communications. Incoming messages flooded the lines and people jammed the lobby, waiting for a short allotment of time to place a call. From their perch just above the scene of the action, the operators had a close and unobstructed view of the rescue efforts, an obvious distraction. But quick thinking on the part of the switchboard supervisor, Pauline Hughes, removed that temptation. Hughes pulled down the window shades and fastened the shutters, blocking out the commotion below. The concerns her subordinates held were legitimate, extending beyond casual curiosity. One operator had a friend in the wreckage, another a cousin—both perished. The six operators on duty, though thoroughly overwhelmed, worked late into the night. Their boss, the president of the Union Telephone Company, Clinton Shock, was also working—as a rescuer. Employees working at the telegraph office across the square were equally busy.

The eight dead included five women, two men and one child. The tallies of the injured, as reported by newspapers, were slightly inconsistent. The published accounts of the number of injured varied, but the majority put the count at thirteen. Most lists excluded Luther Stephenson and the unidentified black porter because they escaped injury early on, but all lists included Vernie Graves, who had also emerged unscathed. Mayor Finch was, of course, pleased that early estimates represented a substantial overstatement of the number of people inside the buildings. Once the count was official, most people viewed the timing as somewhat fortunate, noting that the store had been packed in the morning and that a meeting scheduled in the Odd Fellows hall that evening was expected to draw dozens to the third floor.

Friday was cloudy both figuratively and literally, a day for unrewarding and grueling work. The *Dallas Morning News* characterized the scene and mood that morning, stating, "The morning following the tragedy broke cold and cheerless."[93] It was an apt description. There was still much work to be done within the wide perimeter, but the eager search for living human forms was absent. The cover photo shows a remarkable and frightening scene in which throngs of people climbed on the precarious wreckage the day following the collapse. John McKinney wisely delayed the day's work until late morning, allowing workers time to regain their strength, but it appears he failed to secure the scene from gawkers, many of whom exercised poor judgment. Among the volunteers who came to help that morning was seventy-year-old Cheeves employee Ben Estes.

Scores of volunteers filled wagons with a curious mixture of items consisting of Odd Fellows regalia, rumpled and trodden pieces of inventory and fragments of building materials. As the pile of rubbish began to shrink, the eerie silhouette of the remnants of the buildings came into full view. Surprisingly, there was much intact. The west wall of the Bates Building had withstood the collapse unscathed. The back portions of both stores still stood, both representing later additions to the original structures built in 1876. Jagged pieces of flooring still clung in the corners, extending out far enough that items, even some heavy ones, were still suspended on the shaky remains overhead. Part of a closet belonging to the Odd Fellow hall was laid bare on two sides, while the other sides appeared almost undisturbed. The odd arrangement created a precarious working environment for the volunteers. The *Dallas Morning News* described the scene:

> *The mammoth pile of shattered brick, splintered timber and ruined merchandise has been shifted from the site, except for an unapproachable heap beneath the shaking floors of the ruined implement building from which vehicles and merchandise are being removed with the care and delicacy of touch of an expert playing at jackstraws, and for a similar heap of rubbish on the opposite side of the collapsed department store, considered by the searchers to be beyond the zone of possible bodies.*[94]

Cheeves store manager O.C. Stewart located an empty commercial space where his store's salvageable merchandise could be taken and evaluated. He was fortunate that a grocery store owned by J.M. Andrews had recently relocated, leaving vacant its former space in the Mallow Building on the southwest corner of the square. He secured the space and, finding it suitable for his needs, soon decided that it would serve as the store's new home.

Walter Wilson, operating on little sleep, answered telegrams and worked on special editions of his paper. As always, on Friday evening, the twenty-fourth, he committed his thoughts to his diary: "People are stupefied by disaster of yesterday; all occupation is abandoned. Great crowds of people are in town, special trains and coaches are coming in with people."[95] Wilson believed that the crash came at 3:45 p.m. rather than 3:40 p.m.

The brief two-page entry into Wilson's journal offers some details about his life. Although he owned a large farm/ranch/orchard that he called his Cotton Hill Place, he and his wife, Josie, boarded with his mother-in-law, whom he referred to as Mama. The Wilsons might have lived with Josie's mother, who was recently widowed, to keep her company, or they may have lived there for easy access to Walter's newspaper office. Wilson mentioned a rather surprising fact: several of the funerals were held on the twenty-fourth,

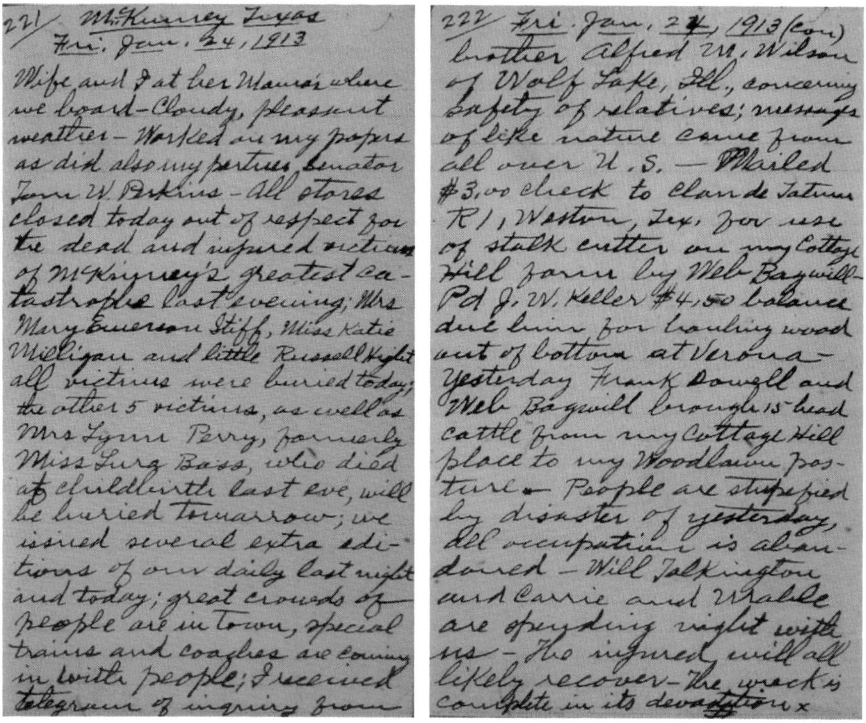

221 McKinney Texas
Fri. Jan. 24, 1913
Wife and I at her Mama's where we board—Cloudy, pleasant weather—Worked on my papers as did also my partners, Senator Tom W. Perkins—All stores closed today out of respect for the dead and injured victims of McKinney's greatest catastrophe last evening; Mrs Mary Emerson Stiff, Miss Katie Milligan and little Russell Hight all victims were buried today; the other 5 victims, as well as Mrs Lynn Perry, formerly Miss Lura Bass, who died at childbirth last eve, will be buried tomorrow; we issued several extra editions of our daily last night and today; great crowds of people are in town, special trains and coaches are coming in with people; I received telegram of inquiry from

222 Fri. Jan. 24, 1913 (con)
brother Alfred M. Wilson of Wolf Lake, Ill., concerning safety of relatives; messages of like nature came from all over U.S.—Mailed $3.00 check to Claude Tatum R1, Weston, Tex. for use of stalk cutter on my Cottage Hill farm by Web Bagwill—Pd J. W. Keller $4.50 balance due him for hauling wood out of bottom at Verona—Yesterday Frank Dowell and Web Bagwill brought 15 head cattle from my Cottage Hill place to my Woodlawn pasture—People are stupefied by disaster of yesterday, all occupation is abandoned—Will Talkington and Carrie and Mable are spending night with us—The injured will all likely recover—The wreck is complete in its devastation x

Walter Wilson's diary, January 24, 1913. *Walter B. Wilson Collection, Briscoe Center for American History, University of Texas at Austin.*

an amazing feat. He also wrote about receiving letters of condolence and inquiry from all over the United States.

Elder Horn, who was John Thomas's father-in-law, also recorded his thoughts on the days following the tragedy, an event he described as "the saddest event ever known to McKinney." Horn wanted to go into town but lamented that it was too muddy for him to make the trip in a buggy.

Some people came to help, but unfortunately, a larger number came to gawk. The numbers created problems both on the night of the collapse and on the day following. Public services, like those of the interurban and communications systems, were strained. Restaurants ran out of food, and hotels turned away many when the interurban was too full to take them home. The temporary morgue was forced to screen visitors, sorting out family members from those who came to view the dead out of morbid curiosity.[96]

News regarding the condition of the injured circulated. Annie Curts, suffering injury and trauma, was hospitalized at the institution belonging to Dr. Joe Largent. She accommodated a reporter with the *Fort Worth Record* who asked for a bedside interview and told him of her ordeal with John Thomas and her fear of being left alone while Thomas tried to help others. She was ready to go home, she told the newsman. Her nerves were raw, having been subjected throughout the night to the unsettling cries of others who were more seriously injured than she.[97]

Iva Kistler was in poor condition, with a broken collarbone and four broken ribs. Her little daughter, Anna, initially reported to have had a broken finger, was reported uninjured in later reports. Iva's mother, Fannie Graves, was suffering from a laceration to her left eye socket as well as other cuts and bruises.

Belle McWilliams was in serious condition, her agony stemming from a serious cut to the head and the effects of being crushed. Lyda Moreland had slight cuts to her face and hands. She marveled at an odd thing she had seen during the ordeal. Lyda had been caught briefly between two heavy showcases that had been jarred from their locations by the force of falling objects, yet the glass in each remained unbroken. Stella Russell and Jennie Barnett were heavily bruised.

Iva Shirley had injuries to her feet and a cut over her right eye that had bled profusely. She said that she, like John Thomas, remembered hearing the tiny of voice of Anna Kistler praying and telling her mother that she was not afraid. Lula Searcy had been seriously crushed and was suffering from shock.

There were also incidental injuries associated with the collapse. Several of the rescuers received minor wounds, and some locals loosely linked another death to the accident. Josiah Hewett, the fifty-eight-year-old new hire working his first day at the Tingle store, had escaped into the street on the day of the accident with his employer. Almost immediately after the accident, Hewett fell ill with pneumonia, and he died the following Wednesday, a mere six days after the accident. Hewett had moved to McKinney from Abilene in advance of his wife to start his new job. Mrs. Hewett was preparing to make the move to McKinney when she was summoned to her husband's deathbed. Some people speculated that the contaminated air had contributed to the unfortunate man's demise.

Local papers were filled with public messages related to the tragedy. Mayor Finch posted this plea and committed it to circulars that were passed around town:

> *Citizens of McKinney: Confronted by the greatest and most heartrending disaster in the history of McKinney, we know you will be quick to respond*

> *to the request that all business houses be closed and all business suspended for the day in order that we may show our respect for the dead and sympathy for those in distress.*[98]

It would seem that a request for a show of respect would have been entirely unnecessary. Not so. Amid the throngs of heroes and Samaritans who offered help lurked a pair of insensitive rapscallions from Dallas who decided to take advantage of McKinney at its most vulnerable time. The story is rather comical but only because it had an appropriate outcome.

Exactly one week following McKinney's misfortune, two clumsy thieves broke into the S.H. Abbott & Sons jewelry store on the northwest corner of the square. It was about midnight when they entered the store and nabbed a tray of rings and bracelets. Not satisfied with their take, the two then moved upstairs to a dental office, where they took some gold filling valued at about ten dollars. A third stop was cut short at the clothing store of Jake Morris when Morris, who was sleeping in a back room, heard the pair trying to unlock his door and scared them away.

City Marshal John McKinney proved that he was as capable at police work as he was at orchestrating a massive rescue effort. Within a week, he had collared the two young men responsible: Schofield Poe and Bas McCown. The pair confessed and later turned the stolen goods over to McKinney's assistant, Constable Will Kerby.[99]

With a few exceptions, the local newspapers in McKinney did a good job of capturing the story of the collapse, reporting the facts accurately and consistently. On the morning of January 30, McKinney residents had a large amount of information to digest. The *Weekly Democrat-Gazette* produced a sixteen-page edition in two sections, while the *McKinney Examiner* published two separate editions on the same day to accommodate the extra material. Information about the catastrophe in the first edition of the *Examiner* was a reprint of the story as the *Dallas Morning News* had published it six days earlier. The decision to print that "not so new" news turned out to be a poor one.[100]

The *Examiner* and the *Democrat-Gazette*, both weeklies, had an advantage when it came to reporting the story because their next editions were not due until January 30, a full week after the accident. The extra days gave them time to obtain measured interviews with the survivors and weed out some misinformation that was circulating. Daily newspapers, especially those rushing to publish the story on the morning of January 24, were vulnerable to errors and were thus the source of some inaccurate and inconsistent reports. Such errors, understandable perhaps, are nonetheless problematic—once published, they are impossible to expunge. For example, a Fort Worth paper bungled John Thomas's story with a string of errors and quotes it attributed to Thomas that were obviously incorrect. By way of example: "I felt Miss Searcy back of me pulling at my foot."[101] The newsman had obviously mixed up the names of Curts and Searcy. The men who actually deserved the credit for freeing Searcy, like Dr. Jonas Knight, were cheated out of the credit, and John Thomas may have felt apologetic, as though he were trying to take more credit than was due him, which was certainly not the case.

Other errors were less excusable. The Fort Worth writer took much liberty with the truth, giving broad credit to Thomas for saving the lives of "sobbing and hysterical" women, including not only Lula Searcy but also Estelle (*sic*) McWilliams.[102] It was a stinging error, considering that Thomas greatly regretted his inability to reach Belle McWilliams. She, like Searcy, was saved by the efforts of several rescuers.

The sentiments of the times were on display in isolated news reports. These glimpses into the mindsets of the day are interesting and sometimes amusing by today's standards, but they are a part of the history. One newspaper, attempting to compliment the female telephone supervisor, published this gem: "The young woman, instead of screaming or fainting, shut the window tightly."[103]

The disaster at McKinney was national news. Reports published in newspapers in other states, however, were sometimes crafted using less caution and more exaggeration. The worst offender was perhaps the *Cleveland Leader*. The *Leader* reported that between eight and fifty people were believed killed, many unidentifiable due to the mutilation of their bodies. The same source reported that several clerks had escaped by jumping from a second-story window and that three Tingle employees had likely met their deaths.[104] The *Elkhart Daily Review*, an Indiana newspaper, reported that a doctor had administered a lethal dose of morphine to Norman Presley.[105] The *Times-Picayune* of New Orleans sensationalized the story using a bold headline that declared women and babies had been crushed.[106]

While the vast majority of the information published about the collapse was fair and accurate, there was one egregious exception. Without naming a source or categorizing the statement as an opinion, *Dallas Morning News* writer Henry L. Marriner offhandedly included a damning and premature conclusion about the cause of the disaster when he wrote, "Pressed outward by the weight of the heavy implements of the stock, the wall of the implement store swayed, sagged, and burst through into the department store."[107]

The story about the Tingle building falling onto its neighbor could be traced to J.C. Moore, who was standing on the courthouse steps when the buildings fell. But Moore, who seemed certain that the Tingle building had fallen first, was not an impartial witness. Moore was not only an Odd Fellow, according to Gideon Dowlen, he had been in charge of overseeing the third-floor addition as well and was in the farm implement business in direct competition with T.J. Tingle.

Walter Wilson had furnished many of the details that appeared in other papers on the evening of the collapse, but he had almost certainly *not* furnished information that put the onus on Tingle. The proof is in his diary. In the early morning hours of January 24, Walter Wilson, after working until midnight, chronicled the details of the horrific day. Never expecting anyone to read his private thoughts, he freely wrote of his opinion as to the cause of the accident, with no mention of the Tingle building.[108] Wilson's exact words on the subject are featured in a later chapter. It is highly unlikely that, just an hour or so before entering his opinion in his diary, Wilson would have wired information that Tingle's heavy inventory had caused the collapse.

But unfortunately, the *McKinney Examiner*, in carelessly reprinting the Marriner story in its first edition the following week, caused an immediate firestorm. Naturally, T.J. Tingle, and possibly others, took umbrage with the assessment. In a subsequent edition on the thirtieth, the *Examiner* apologized for the reference and for other errors that had been published by the *News*, then unwittingly republished in the *Examiner*.[109] The editor called the errors unfortunate, stating that the *News* had apologized, and ensured readers that the paper held no ill will toward T.J. Tingle. It also invited readers to take note of a statement running in the same issue on Tingle's behalf, probably at no cost. That note said:

> *The report in effect and believed by some that I had my second floor overloaded and containing heavy implements is incorrect.* ***I have no implements at all on*** **[the]** ***section of*** **[the]** ***second floor that collapsed*** [bold type original] *not exceeding 15,000 pounds of vehicles, and all of them set up, except 8 jobs, in a space of 30x110 feet. I hope no reasonable person, after taking all the facts into consideration, will conclude that the building occupied by me or the stock I had on hand, had anything to do with the sad catastrophe. I suggest that we all forget it near as possible and thank our Maker that it was no worse than it was.*[110]

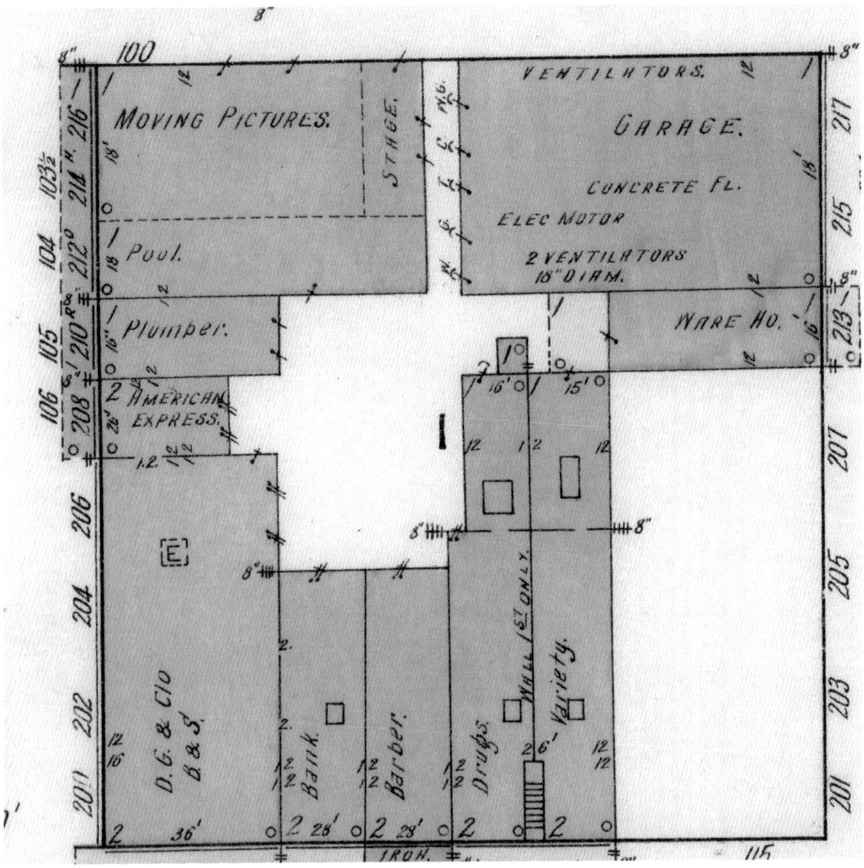


This 1914 Sanborn map of the north side of the town square shows empty lots where the stores once stood. *Courtesy of the Briscoe Center for American History, University of Texas at Austin.*

It was natural for T.J. Tingle to feel defensive, but it seems unlikely that the above statement garnered him any support. To make matters worse, Tingle's awkward defense appeared in the same column with the Cheeves brothers' expression of compassion and sorrow for the community, along with other well-crafted public expressions of sympathy. Tingle might have done well to stop one sentence short when preparing his dispatch. Certainly, at that early stage, no one was in a mood to forget.

# 11
# MOVING FORWARD

There was, of course, more than a little unease about the subject of blame. T.J. Tingle was in a most unenviable position. If there was to be a fight—and there *was*—he was pitted against the Odd Fellows, a large group of influential men who were unceasingly loyal to one another, and the savvy, well-financed and well-connected Cheeves brothers. He had few allies, was relatively new to the area and was working under a contract with Avery and Sons that had suddenly become onerous. Tingle, as an agent, sold Avery's products under a consignment agreement that spelled out his obligations unequivocally. Equipment in his possession was under his protective care, leaving him liable for the inventory damaged in the collapse. According to the agreement, he had thirty days to pay Avery for the lost inventory.[111]

Within a week of the collapse, Tingle had placed a large ad in the *Examiner*, inviting potential customers to see a load of implements that had just arrived at his new store on North Kentucky Street. Whether or not Tingle intended to stay in McKinney, he needed to sell a large number of buggies and equipment not damaged in the catastrophe as well as new inventory that had been en route when the accident occurred. He continued to run ads until May, when he was compelled to transfer the remaining inventory to Sid H. Brown, another local Avery dealer in McKinney.[112] Thomas Tingle, his wife, Grace, and the couple's children who still lived at home moved to Muskogee, Oklahoma.

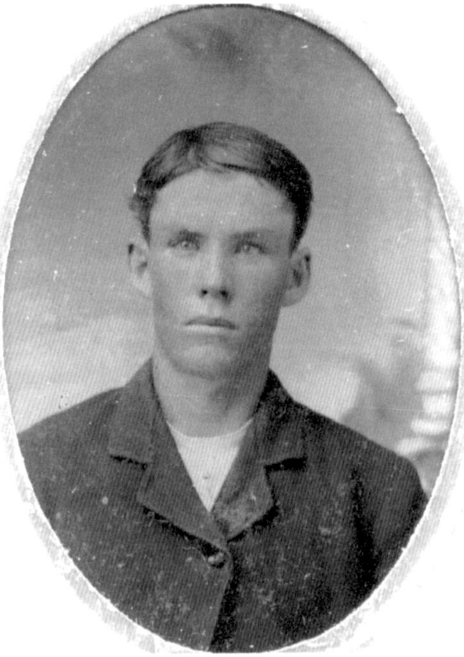

Ike Talkington, contractor, as a young man. *Courtesy of David Miller.*

In view of the conclusions drawn and published against him, Tingle had understandably reacted defensively after the accident. So, too, had a group of workmen who had worked on the Odd Fellows building just days before the collapse. Members of the group, consisting of Ike Talkington, C.M. Brantley, Fred Owenby and W.G. Ashley, felt they needed to counter an accusatory rumor that was circulating. They did so by crafting and releasing a statement to the paper over their signatures. Charles Isaac "Ike" Talkington, the contractor on the job, was the first to sign.

A week before the collapse, the workmen had replaced a wood, lathe and plaster ceiling on the third story of the Odd Fellows building with a metal one. According to the men's disclaimer, rumors were swirling that they had weakened the structure while making that change, either by chiseling into the brick or by adding excess weight to the upper portion of the building. The men answered their accusers in the *Examiner* with these words:

> *A rumor has gained currency that the walls of the Odd Fellows building, which collapsed with such fatal results, were weakened by being chiseled into and some brick removed from them by the workmen who took down the plastered ceiling of the third story and substituted therefore a metal ceiling, thus contributing to some degree, more or less, to the deplorable disaster. In*

> *regard to this rumor, we the workmen who were employed to do the job by the trustees of the Odd Fellows' Lodge, wish to publicly state in print that such are not the facts. The walls of the building were in nowise molested by us. They were not cut into, not a brick taken out nor even the plaster on the wall cracked or broken anywhere. The few bricks and bats taken out by us were found between the plaster ceiling of the second floor and the plank floor of the lodge room, or third story, which brick and bats had evidently been left there by the workmen when the third story was added more than twenty years ago. We might further state, for the public information, that the plaster and lathe ceiling removed was much heavier in weight than the ceiling substituted therefore by us. Thus, the result of our work lessened, rather than increased the weight and strain on the walls of the ill-fated building.*[113]

Similar rumors about the Bates Building rippled through the community. The accusations took on a familiar refrain—joists had been cut and so forth. In the case of the Bates Building, the damage had allegedly been done when Tingle installed an elevator and skylight. Every suggestion that attempted to assign blame had a common theme: the accident was predictable and preventable.

Chief John McKinney made this rather chilling statement to a newspaper soon after the collapse:

> *I've been told, before this calamity took place, that the building was unsafe. I discussed it with various people, but they declared that it had been passed on by a committee of architects something like fifteen years ago, when the third story was added and had been pronounced safe. I don't know whether this is true or not. I know that there are other persons who have said that the building was unsafe.*[114]

The third floor had actually been added twenty-two years earlier, and the chief's vague references to unnamed "people" were of little value. There was a lot of this kind of shoulder shrugging.

Gideon Dowlen added more troubling comments to the pool of speculation. Dowlen had firsthand knowledge of the building and its structural soundness (or lack thereof). He had finished the third-floor addition in 1891 after the architect, William S. Sterrett, quit the job. Dowlen offered no explanation for Sterrett's exit, but he was happy to share his own opinion about the addition. He always believed, he told a newspaper, that the building was too light to carry a third story. It is hard to imagine why Dowlen made such statements for the record. Not only had he done the work despite his reservations, but Gideon Dowlen had also been a city alderman in 1891—and thus was in a position to do something about the threat to public safety. Dowlen had apparently carried that concern for twenty-two years without acting on it.[115]

Dowlen also stated the obvious. The rear portions of both buildings that remained standing were additions made to enlarge the original 1876 structures. The added footage to the Bates Building was done in 1902, and the add-on for the Odd Fellows building was done between 1876 and 1891. Dowlen opined that the intact walls would be hard to dislodge, and his assessment proved true. Workers had to use dynamite to bring the back walls down.

The tidal wave of help and sympathy that came after the accident was followed by a swell of subtle censure. The *Beaumont Enterprise* published this opinion: "The lesson to be learned from the collapse of one of McKinney's principal business buildings is plain enough. In the absence of an adequate and uniform building law in the State, it is possible to patch up structures that are a menace to the public."[116]

A spokesman for the City of Fort Worth appeared somewhat insensitive to McKinney's wounded pride when he gloated about Fort Worth's building codes. He stated that while other towns were hurriedly inspecting buildings in the wake of the McKinney ordeal, such action was not necessary in Fort Worth, where a routine inspection policy and strict rules regarding construction were already in place. The city building inspector in Dallas had quite the opposite comment, admitting that Dallas had many public buildings in need of work. He lamented that his attention was spread thin, as he tried to attend to the myriad problems associated with aging buildings.

A letter sent to Mayor Finch by the mayor of Denton showed just how unsophisticated and arbitrary the process of assessing structural safety was in Texas in 1913. To his credit, Mayor Edmond Bates hoped to take lessons from McKinney's sorrowful event that he might use to protect his own citizenry. He asked for Finch's opinion about the cause of the structural failures, inquiring specifically about the thickness of the shared wall. He added, "Sometimes I think it hard to condemn public buildings, and have refrained from taking such steps, but this horror at McKinney reminds me of an obligation to the living that cannot be settled with money."[117]

Mayor Finch was well aware that some degree of public criticism would surface, and some would be confined to whispers. Almost immediately after the accident, he announced, "Inspections of all public buildings will be made promptly and regularly, including the school houses, to ascertain the condition of walls and floors and dead-weight strain."[118] The mayor made good on that promise. By January 31, Henry J. Emmins, the city building inspector for Dallas, had made an inspection of many of the buildings in McKinney and issued a report to the mayor and commissioners outlining his findings. His report stated that he had made a hurried inspection of the older buildings and "those buildings looked upon with suspicion by some of your citizens." Unfortunately for the mayor, Emmins dispensed the kind of noncommittal report that had frustrated members of the school district. The report stated that there was, in his opinion, "no building in a dangerous condition." Yet one paragraph later, Emmins summarized his findings using these words: "Now I do not want you to understand me to say that the conditions of the buildings of your city are not in want of attention, for on the contrary, you have quite a lot of very bad conditions, which can be and should be remedied."[119]

A public confirmation of the collective approval of Mayor Finch's handling of the crisis came from the voting public. He and McKinney's two city commissioners, J.W. Barnes and S.J. Massie, were reelected in early April 1913. It was apparently a time when politics was not at the forefront of public concern. A mere 137 locals cast votes in the election.

Shortly after the accident, the secretary for the lodge, a fellow named Adams, reported his assessment of the monetary damages the local chapter had suffered as a result of the collapse. He placed a value of $12,000 on the building and $5,000 on lost furniture and paraphernalia. The group carried insurance against fire loss but none that would cover the collapse. T.J. Tingle estimated the value of his lost inventory at about $8,000, for which he had $4,000 worth of insurance. He estimated the value of the building, which still belonged to the Bates children, at $10,000. Tingle had been fortunate enough to recover his books and records from the wreckage. The Cheeves loss, originally estimated at between $75,000 and $100,000, was later revised to between $50,000 and $60,000.

Oscar Stewart announced plans to reopen his Cheeves store on February 20 at its new location in the Mallow Building. The first order of business was a sale of the salvaged inventory. The goods needed to be cleared out, he stated, to make room for shipments of merchandise en route, orders that had been placed before the accident. He also assured the public that Vernie Graves, Ben Estes, John Thomas, Belle McWilliams and Lula Searcy would remain on staff. The Odd Fellows resumed their regular business, using the facilities of a local church as their meeting hall.

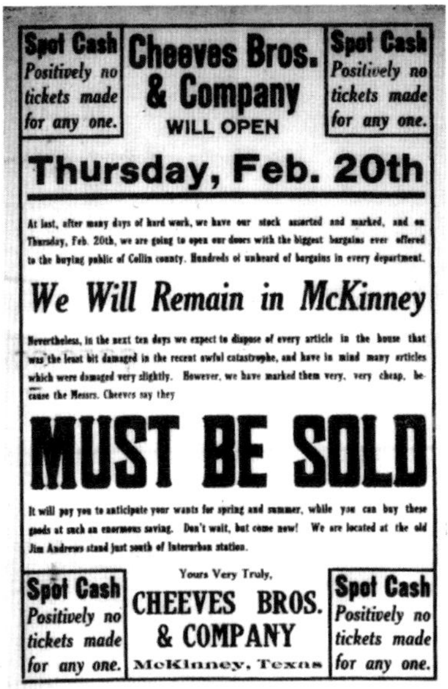


The Cheeves store announces its reopening and sale of salvaged inventory. *The* Weekly Democrat-Gazette *(McKinney)*.

Soon after the accident, the lodge displayed a large degree of optimism about its future, when leaders began negotiations with the Bates heirs to buy their McKinney property. The sale of lots 1, 2 and 7 in block 1—lot 7 being the vacant lot on which the Bates Building had stood—closed on April 27, 1913.

On October 1, 1913, eight months after the tragic fall, the citizens of McKinney, by a ratio of more than four to one, voted to adopt a new city charter. The bond limit under the old regime had been reached, making it an impediment to progress. The vote was viewed as a demand for better school facilities, improved public utilities and an expansion of other public improvements, including improved sidewalks, parks and roads. Voters understood the implications; taxes would have to be raised.[120] Walter Wilson celebrated the progress he had long championed.

Signs that things were returning to normal in McKinney were plentiful by the end of summer. In October, merchants and volunteers participated in a massive cleanup day to heighten the visual appeal of the downtown square, where two empty lots served as reminders of the tragedy. Residents still honored the memory of those lost, but they were looking forward rather than back, eager to continue the progress that had been temporarily stalled. A tribute to local businesses that appeared in the *Weekly Democrat-Gazette* on April 9, 1914, highlighted the longevity of McKinney's Cheeves store but made no mention of the tragedy. A $405,000 bond proposal, offered in support of a good roads movement, carried by a vote of 726 to 249.

The year 1914 saw many changes and additions to the landscape of public buildings in McKinney. A new water and electric light plant were built, and even the old jail was remodeled and enlarged. Mayor Finch insisted that a representative with the State Insurance Commission make a thorough inspection of the new power plant. The facility drew a glowing report.

A new high school, built during 1914, opened early the following year. A scarcity of skilled labor and weather delays pushed the estimated completion date back more than once, but a focus on tough building standards outweighed all other concerns. Caddo Construction Company, headquartered in Muskogee, Oklahoma, had a solid track record, a large base of customers and a reputation for using modern construction equipment. Local newspapers boasted that the builders promised, and delivered, a deep and broad foundation that was reinforced with steel rods.[121] The implication was unmistakable; construction of public buildings undertaken in McKinney after January 23, 1913, would bear the highest levels of structural scrutiny. When complete, Boyd High School was a source of great pride and confidence for the city. In early May 1916, another large bond issue carried in support of a new East Ward School.

The terrible catastrophe of 1913 united McKinney residents, who came together and did what was necessary to survive their personal losses and a collective setback. They grieved together and were moving forward together. Unfortunately, there was some unfinished business that was destined to tear some relationships asunder.

# 12
# THE BLAME GAME

The suits and counter suits in the case of the collapsed buildings were long in coming but plentiful. The dozen attorneys involved cast their nets wide, perhaps hoping to tap into some deep pockets. The deepest sets of pockets belonged to the Avery and Sons Plow Company, the large and well-known implement company headquartered in Louisville, Kentucky. One petition also attempted to cast blame on the Grand Lodge of the Odd Fellows in Dallas, without success. The suits took their respective places on the docket, but the fate of each hung largely on the outcome of the first or, more specifically, the jury's verdict in the Presley case. That case, number 19028, was filed on Thursday, January 21, 1915, in the Forty-Fourth District Court in Dallas under this legal title: *Sophy Presley, ET AL vs. Cheeves Bros. & Co., ET AL.* Other defendants in the Presley suit were Avery and Sons, T.J. Tingle and McKinney's Local Empire Lodge No. 68.[122]

The plaintiffs in the Presley suit were Sophia; her five-year-old daughter, Emma Lou; and Norman Presley's aged parents, Emma Jane and Robert Fulton Presley. Sophia asked the court for damages totaling $40,000 to cover the loss of her husband's wages, the family's only source of income. She bore the usual expenses of a single parent but also labored under concern for Emma Lou, who was afflicted with a serious hearing impairment.

Norman's parents, Robert Fulton "R.F." and Emma Jane Presley of Bowie, had added their names to the suit, asking for a small sum to compensate them for money that Norman routinely sent in their support. The compensation they sought, as well as the amount Sophia was seeking on behalf of her daughter, was included in the $40,000 sum she hoped to secure. Although Norman made just $50 per month, the equivalent of $1,237.15 today, he had, for a long period of time, sent a portion of his earnings to his parents. Dallas attorney Daniel Upthegrove represented the Presleys.

It was evident from the beginning that the lodge would shoulder the greatest burden in terms of the need for defense, and it was equally evident, at least to those close to the situation, that Empire Lodge No. 68 intended to battle its accusers without restraint. The petition filed on January 21, 1915, was not the first—or the second—version of the Presley charges. Twice, attorneys for the lodge had pushed back, answering the charges with a complaint of vagueness:

> *Said First Amended Original Petition is too vague, indefinite and uncertain, in that, it does not specifically specify, itemize and designate, as required by law, the grounds upon which negligence is therein charged against this defendant, and by such failure to do so, this defendant is not and cannot be, apprized of the character of the proof it will be called upon to meet in the trial of the said cause.*[123]

Having exhausted every reasonable attempt to stall, attorneys for the lodge finally submitted a lengthy response to the amended charges leveled against their clients in a document that represented a firm denial of "each and every allegation."[124] The denunciations covered a broad range of topics but centered on the condition of the building and the party responsible for the collapse. Lodge representatives stated that the greater portion of the building's space was leased—a circumstance they believed rendered them blameless. As a basis, they claimed that they, as landlords, did not have, "the right of voluntary inspection or control of ownership."[125] They denied knowledge of the building's poor condition and placed the responsibility for maintenance on the Cheeves enterprise, supporting their claim with a statement that a Cheeves representative had inspected the building prior to signing the lease. They also denied claims made by Cheeves that they had failed to deliver on promised repairs.

In answer to the accusation that they had neglected to properly erect and maintain the building, lodge leaders responded that they were not qualified to assess the adequacy of the foundation and walls of the building and had therefore relied on the advice of architects and engineers. They outlined the lodge's agreement with Peter Turbitt, who constructed the common wall in 1876, adding that Turbitt had done the work according to the specifications of and under the supervision of an architect. They spent several pages of their response touting the workmanship and materials that were used, declaring that the property should have had a life of one hundred years. Comments contained in the response, as they related to the 1891 addition, reflected the same confidence and optimism. The assertions the lodge made were replete with references to joists, iron and wooden columns, supports, iron rods, bolts, braces and the "very best" timber, cement and brick, "properly apportioned and proportioned."[126]

While the lodge went to great lengths to extol the excellent standards under which its spokesmen believed the building had been erected and enlarged, the group also mentioned that the Bates Building had been expanded in 1902, when Lea Bates, who had since died, owned the property. Lodge members stated that they were unable to say if the work had been done properly, even though it seemed a moot point, given that much of that portion of the building was still standing after the collapse. While they claimed to have had no knowledge of the quality of the Bates Building's addition, representatives for the lodge seemed well versed about drainage problems that occurred on the Bates property, describing in detail how guttering and spouts were lacking or clogged. The problem, they claimed, had existed for a number of years, causing water to pool behind the Bates Building and seep into the shared wall, weakening it. "This defendant knows and believes that [this situation] caused the collapse of the said building, and that the same was unknown to this defendant, or any of its members or trustees, but could be known to the occupants of the Bates Building by the exercise of reasonable care."[127] The representatives failed to explain how they had acquired a full understanding of the alleged drainage problems only *after* the building was gone.

In addition to the problems wrought by the spouts, the lodge alleged that the Avery Company and T.J. Tingle had stored crates of heavy equipment on the east side of the second floor and allowed them to lean against the shared wall. The second story of the Bates Building had been built to accommodate offices and "sleeping apartments," they stated, not designed to carry heavy weight. Tingle had also weakened the building's support while installing an elevator and skylight, they charged. Their conclusion was thus: the negligence of the Avery company and T.J. Tingle had caused Presley's death. "These defendants say that if the said Norman Presley received injuries as alleged in plaintiff's amended original petition and died as a result thereof, the same were not caused by any negligence on the part of these defendants."[128]

Also in defense of a charge that negligence on the part of the building's owners had endangered Norman Presley's life, the pleadings contained this response:

> *He was in a position to know and did know, better than anyone else, of the real condition of the said building, being employed therein at the time of the collapse of said building, by the said Cheeves Brothers & Company, and for a long time prior thereto, and, in entering and remaining in said building under the circumstances and conditions, this defendant says that the deceased did assume all of the risks incident to his said employment, and the survivor and heirs of the said decedent are therefore not entitled, either by law nor in equity, to recover from this defendant anything of value whatsoever.*

The lodge went even further, stating that Presley, in going into the building when he knew it was unsafe, was "guilty of contributory negligence."[129]

In addition to their written response to the charges, lodge representatives had another grievance and request they wished to lodge. When outlining the charges and making a plea for damages, Sophia Presley had characterized her husband as "kind, affectionate, and dutiful."[130] Attorneys for the lodge objected, asking that in the event the case went to trial, the information be withheld from the jury because it had no relevance to the specific charges.

As a consequence of these delays and amendments, the Presley case did not go to trial until late September 1916. Judge E.B. Muse ruled early on that the charges, as they pertained to Avery and Sons and T.J. Tingle, were without merit, leaving the lodge to battle the Presleys before a jury. It also ended the hopes of the Cheeves owners and lodge members, who had filed petitions against Tingle seeking damages of $30,000 each.

At trial, the old, tired and all-too-familiar accusations that had been circulating for two years were hashed and rehashed before a jury. Many people who had been deposed, requiring them to answer questions in writing, were called as witnesses. Their pretrial statements allowed the attorneys to formulate their plans, preparing questions that would elicit testimony favorable to their argument. Naturally, the subject that dominated the testimony was the condition of the Odd Fellows building, a topic with many tentacles. Among the witnesses called was Lula Searcy, who testified that on the day before the collapse, January 22, 1913, carpenters had been working on the front doors of the Cheeves store because they had become increasingly difficult to open and close. Discussion about the doors supported a broader theme mentioned by Searcy, and echoed by others in their testimony, that drawers and cabinets inside the store did not close properly because the building was so badly out of line. Attorneys also asked Lula about her experience on the day of the accident. She testified that she had seen Vernie Graves escape through a back window just seconds before falling debris forced her to the floor and covered her.

By far, the most damaging testimony to the lodge came from carpenters and other workmen who had worked on the building. Several such men, including those who had replaced the third-floor ceiling just days before the collapse, were among those required to submit written depositions before the trial. As each took his turn in the witness chair, a troubling picture began to emerge. It was perhaps difficult and embarrassing for the men to testify, especially those who were current and former members of the Odd Fellows, a group known for fostering strong bonds. Four workers who had installed the new ceiling just ten days before the collapse had submitted an open letter to the newspaper after the fall, hoping to squelch rumors that they were at fault (see letter on page 94). They were forced to admit under oath that there was much more to the story than their letter had suggested.[131]

According to some of the testimony, the poor condition of the building was so outrageous that the subject became fodder for jokes and ridicule. A craftsman named W.G. Ashley had, while working on the Odd Fellows building, voiced his concern to Ike Talkington and C.M. Brantley, the supervisors on the ceiling job. Ashley told the men that over his many years of doing carpentry work, he had seen some bad things, but he had never seen walls in a worse state than those of the Odd Fellows building. Nails could be driven into the bricks with ease, while the mortar that held them in place crumbled to the touch. Nothing was flush. Floors sagged. Ashley was among the men who had signed his name to the disclaimer about the new ceiling, yet he was compelled to offer full disclosure in court. In particular, he attested to the fact that the bricks were very dry, a point that countered charges against Tingle that his faulty gutters had caused the bricks to remain wet almost constantly.

L.H. Cantwell, a painter and paperhanger, also testified about the problems the building's poor alignment posed. He had been forced to piece together wallpaper to fit the odd angles and to fill gaps when working on the building. Windows that should have had identical measurements differed by several inches due to sagging joists. Cantwell claimed that he had spoken to Ike Talkington about the issues, but the foreman was already aware of the problem and was busy dealing with other similar issues. According to Cantwell, Talkington had expressed a need to replace a supporting column that had, at some earlier time, been removed from inside the Cheeves store, but he claimed that O.C. Stewart, the manager of the store, had balked because he needed the valuable floor space. The dispirited worker (Cantwell) responded by assuring Talkington that it didn't really matter—one or two columns weren't sufficient to solve the building's structural problems anyway.

There was much discussion in the courtroom about unstable floors, in particular, the floor on the third level that vibrated heavily when the Odd Fellows held ceremonial marches. L.W. Mayhew, one of the workers and a former Odd Fellow, had painted the new ceiling. He said he was uneasy about the middle portion of the ceiling because it sagged severely. Mayhew also admitted that discussions about the third floor—and more specifically the wisdom of having made that addition—were topics of frequent discussion among lodge members.

F.C. Hogg was another paperhanger who was called to testify about work he had done on the third floor. Like the others, he had marveled at the condition of the structure and recalled that wallpaper cut to fit one side of the building was five inches too long to fit the opposite side.

Workers also talked about a crack that had grown over time in the exterior east wall. The crack had become something of a conversation piece, extending downward from the third floor, where it had grown to an estimated length between ten and fifteen feet. The crack had also been the source of some lighthearted discussions that eventually lost any semblance of humor. A storeowner named Walter Howell relayed the details of a conversation he had one day with O.C. Stewart while standing outside the Cheeves store. According to Howell, Stewart told him about his plans to improve his store, but the changes he mentioned were purely cosmetic. Howell testified that he pointed to the large crack and suggested that it might make more sense to tear the place down and start over. Howell quoted Stewart as having replied, "Well it has been there a long time, and nothing has happened yet."[132]

The depositions supplied the attorneys with valuable information, much of which they wanted to have witnesses repeat before the jury. The most efficient way for them to ensure that witnesses did not soften or modify their initial statements was to use the witnesses' words, restated in the form of a question. The attorneys employed this technique, often beginning or ending

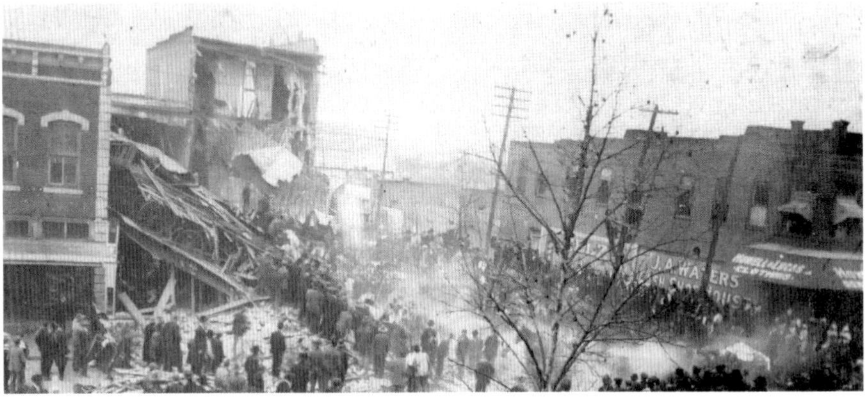


Shot showing the location of the Howell & Lucas and Waters stores in proximity to the Cheeves building. *Courtesy of Bob Patterson.*

questions with the phrase: "Isn't it a fact that…" The exercise was purely for the benefit of the jury and the record, but it was effective.

Although the collective testimony of the workmen was likely the deciding factor for jury members in arriving at their verdict, the testimony of one particular witness, who was not a workman, deserves mention. Several men had witnessed the collapse from a variety of locations that afternoon, each having a slightly unique perspective due to the angle with which he viewed the collapse. But there had been no consensus among the witnesses as to which wall had been the first to fall. Walter Howell, mentioned earlier as the owner of a menswear store named Howell & Lucas, was among those eyewitnesses. His statement, if accurate, removes doubt as to the origin point of the collapse. Howell had been standing in front of Waters' Shoe store just seconds before the catastrophe on the afternoon of January 23, talking with store owner James Waters. As he walked back to his store, Howell said that he heard a noise and looked up.

Sophia Presley's attorney, crafting his question using information from Howell's deposition, ensured that the wording was just as Howell had originally stated it.

> *You were standing out in front of the store, and saw the building when it fell and it fell in this manner: the top story of the Odd Fellow's building collapsed and fell in first, and this seemed to cause something like combustion, that is it caused the objects to be thrown out the windows in the second floor in the front of the building, and immediately after the third floor collapsed and fell in, the 1st and 2nd floors fell in.…Isn't this a fact?*[133]

Several days after the trial ended, the *Democrat-Gazette* published the verdict, characterizing the judgment as one of the biggest ever returned in district court in Dallas, adding, "The case was on trial nearly three weeks, twelve attorneys were employed, and it was stubbornly fought all the way through."[134]

Indeed, it had been.

# 13
# WHEN GOOD MEN DID NOTHING

As the end of the trial drew near, it must have been rather clear that the jury was going to deliver a verdict unfavorable to the lodge. Hoping to end any need for further litigation with the Presley family, the Cheeves owners offered—and Sophia Presley accepted—a settlement of $5,000. On September 26, Presley dismissed the charges against the Cheeves brothers and O.C. Stewart, agreeing that she would take no future action against the storeowners in the matter.

The remaining Dallas-based cases, languishing in the Sixty-Eighth District Court, were also soon dismissed or settled. They consisted of a suit brought by R.L. and Lelia Hight, asking for damages of $7,000, and one brought by Mr. and Mrs. R.G. Milligan, also seeking $7,000. The two families dismissed all defendants in their suits expect for the lodge, each agreeing to accept $1,500 from Empire No. 68.[135] Two other cases, filed in the Fifty-Ninth District Court in Sherman, were not decided until October, but they, too, ended with judgments against the lodge. Mary Emerson Stiff's two young sons were awarded $9,000, and Lula Bush, the widow of Leslie Bush, was awarded $6,000 on behalf of her youngest daughter, also named Leslie.[136]

As part of their deliberations, members of the jury were instructed to answer a list of specific questions related to the condition of the Odd Fellows building and to express their collective opinion as to whether or not the structure had been properly constructed and maintained. Their answers were unequivocal; Empire No. 68 had been woefully negligent in accessing and attending to structural problems. The jury returned its verdict on

Thursday, September 28, 1916, awarding the Presleys $21,000 (in addition to the $5,000 paid them by the Cheeves owners) and also awarding "all costs of the suit." Of the total $26,000, they allotted $15,000 of the judgment to Sophia, $10,000 to young Emma Lou and $1,000 to Norman's mother, Emma Jane.[137]

Members of Empire No. 68 wasted no time announcing that they would seek protection under bankruptcy laws. "The lodge has suffered so many reverses and has been under a cloud so long that it was thought that it could not be successfully continued," wrote the *Democrat-Gazette*. During the last week of October, trustees J.L. Franklin, George Wilcox and F.B. Pope, acting on behalf of Empire No. 68, filed a voluntary petition in bankruptcy with the federal district court in Sherman. The petition listed assets in the amount of $15,704.30 and liabilities totaling $44,001.94. A message accompanying the petition consisted of this single, extremely long sentence:

> *Whereas, based on the calamity which befell Empire Lodge #68 of the Independent Order of the Odd Fellows of McKinney, Texas, by the collapse of their building on the 23rd of January, 1913 there has been rendered in a district court in Dallas county, a judgment in favor of Emma Lou Pressley* [sic] *et al, for the sum of $21,000 and said lodge is indebted to other parties in the amount of $8,500, secured by a lien upon the real estate of the lodge, and other suits are now pending for two other cases, said lodge is entirely unable to pay said amounts, and has no property out of which any considerable portion of such sums can be paid, and being desirous of relieving itself of future burdens and liability on account of such judgment and claims and being desirous of continuing its work, duties, aims and obligations in the future by availing itself of the provisions of the federal bankruptcy laws of the United States.*[138]

As a condition of the bankruptcy, the federal court in Sherman took control of the lodge's remaining assets, which included both of the vacant lots where the stores had once stood, the lodge having purchased the Bates lot a few months after the collapse. Court-appointed referee Charles Batsell of Sherman met with creditors during the third week of November 1916, just prior to the liquidation of assets, and he placed an estimate of their collective value at $15,000. To the surprise of Tom Tinnison, the trustee who facilitated the sale by sealed bid, the notoriety of the real estate had elevated its value. Eight McKinney residents offered bids ranging from $14,500 to the winning bid of $18,000. The highest bidder was a woman named

Henrietta Wilson. "Etta" Wilson was the widow of Thomas B. Wilson, a prosperous engineer who had accomplished much before his death in 1913, including being party to the 1909 buyout of the Continental Bank and Trust Company, which was renamed the Continental State Bank. Years earlier, Thomas Wilson had also helped organize the Collin County National Bank, which he served as a director. By investing in the commercial property, Etta Wilson was continuing a practice her husband had followed during his life. The couple's adult son, Addison (1892–1970), also following his father's lead, served as president of McKinney's Central State Bank.[139]

F.B. Pope secured the remaining items of lodge paraphernalia with an offer of $105. Pope had also bid on the lot. It took several months for the lodge to wrap up its business, but in late August 1917, Empire Lodge No. 68 was dissolved, its charter surrendered.

The *Democrat-Gazette* published a tribute to Empire No. 68, a sort of obituary, in which it praised the group's sixty-two years of good work. The order had sought to carry out the principles of the organization, which included elevating the character of man and enlarging the sphere of his usefulness, the *Gazette* stated. The Odd Fellows had supported the cause of educating and housing orphans, cared for widows and conducted many funerals, with a goal of relieving the distressed. "But a distress had finally come upon the lodge that has taken its life."[140] So said the *Gazette*.

There was actually little need for a farewell message to honor the memory of McKinney's Odd Fellows, because the group had disbanded in name only. Members were simply operating under a new number and under a new (and hopefully more sound) roof. On January 15, 1917, a full eight months before the old lodge was officially dissolved, a new chapter, the W.C. Burrus No. 953, was officially organized in McKinney. The order was named for a longtime miller who had been an Odd Fellow for over fifty years before his death. The new Odd Fellows hall was located behind the old location, where it remained in use until the group's 1943 dissolution. The Odd Fellows insignia still marks the building.

It is impossible and unnecessary to attempt to assign blame for this tragedy to any specific individuals. Officers in the Odd Fellows organization came and went over the years. But without question, a slew of otherwise good men had ignored the obvious for a long time.

The collapse was, of course, an accident. It is interesting to contemplate that members of the lodge could just as easily have been the victims if the timing had been different. Although they had vehemently and publically denied a scintilla of wrongdoing, the leaders of the lodge undoubtedly regretted that they had failed to address the building's problems, with lethal results. Their actions before the court are a different subject. It is doubtful that, during and after the trial, the local citizenry knew much about the lodge's actions in court. If bruised feelings spilled out beyond the courtroom and into the community, there is no record of it. Newspapers were silent about the unpleasant aspects of the trial, making only broad statements like the one that characterized the trial as "stubbornly fought." And today, it seems that few McKinney residents even know that litigation comprised the final chapter of the story of the fallen buildings.

In the end, it was the testimony of many that led the jury to place the blame squarely on decision makers within the Odd Fellows local group. Witnesses, who undertook their duty under the law to testify truthfully, even though it placed them within an embarrassing circle of negligence, exposed the sad truth.

With a comprehensive version of the story now compiled for the historical record, it is proper that we continue to place the memory of these victims above all else, remembering that many lives were cut short or severely altered on that cold afternoon in January in McKinney, Texas.

## THOSE KILLED

| | |
|---|---|
| Leslie Bush | male shopper |
| Russell Hight | four-year-old child in the store with Stella Russell |
| Kate Milligan | customer |
| Robert Norman Presley | clerk |
| Eva Searcy | clerk and sister to Lula Searcy |
| Mary Emerson Stiff | clerk |
| Bessie Wade | customer |
| Rosa Welch | customer |

## THOSE INJURED AND THOSE WHO ESCAPED WITHOUT INJURY

| | |
|---|---|
| Jennie Barnett | customer |
| Annie Curts | clerk |

| | |
|---|---|
| Fannie Graves | customer |
| Vernie Graves | clerk |
| Annie Kistler | four-year-old child |
| Iva Kistler | customer |
| Belle McWilliams | clerk |
| Lyda Moreland | customer |
| Stella Russell | customer |
| Lula Searcy | cashier |
| Cassie Seay | customer |
| Iva Shirley | customer |
| Luther Stephenson | delivery boy |
| John Thomas | manager of dress goods |
| Unidentified porter | |

(a newspaper report about two unidentified female shoppers who made an immediate escape could not be verified)

# 14

# AFTERWARD AND AFTERTHOUGHTS

In late 1917, construction began on a new building on the old Odd Fellows lot that would serve as the new quarters for McKinney's Central State Bank. The bank only had a short distance to move, having been located just a few doors west of its new location for many years. Central State Bank had experienced several changes since its founding in McKinney on June 1, 1906, beginning as Continental Bank and Trust, changing to Continental State Bank in 1909 and Central State Bank in 1917. Cognizant of the lot's sad history, and perhaps expecting extra scrutiny, the builders ensured that the new structure was made of fireproof material and reinforced concrete floors. Instead of a third floor, the new edifice included a full basement that featured a pair of separate entrances at street level. It also had an innovative enclosed stairwell that originated outside, leading to the second floor. The new structure, complete by May 1918, quartered the bank at ground level, office space for professionals on the second floor and a barber in the basement. The building served the bank until 1963, when the institution moved to a location off the square, likely to facilitate a new trend in "motor banking," which required space for a drive-up window.

Today, a store filled with antiques, collectibles and other treasures operates out of the old bank building, one of many charming stores on the old court square. The wooden floors and the massive vaults in the back of the store are reminiscent of the building's recent history but still highlight its nostalgic charm. The building, although nearing the century mark, is actually among the newer structures on the square.

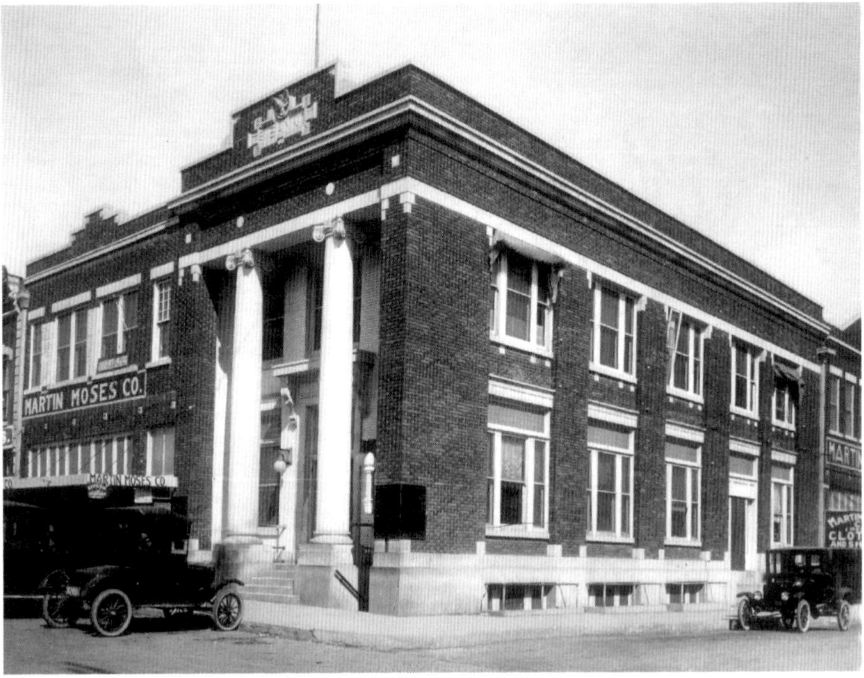


New bank building before the bank sign was installed. *Courtesy of Collin County Historical Museum.*

The McKinney Cheeves store continued to operate under the management of Oscar Stewart until early 1919, when he was forced to retire due to poor health. Ed Pettus, of Dallas, purchased interest in the Cheeves store and took over the management on February 1, 1919. Pettus made considerable improvements to the store, including the addition of a balcony, enlarged storefront windows and modern lighting. Pettus reported that 1919 had been a banner year for the store. Having almost doubled its business over the previous year, it was approaching annual sales of $250,000.[141] Oscar Stewart, who had managed the Cheeves store for sixteen years, died at age forty-seven on March 26, 1920, from tuberculosis. He and wife Annie had no children.

Thomas J. Tingle and his wife lived out the remainder of their lives in Muskogee, where Thomas worked as a bookkeeper for an automobile dealership and as a salesman. He died in 1940 at age seventy-nine, just ten months after losing his wife, Grace. At the time of their deaths, the couple's six children had blessed them with eleven grandchildren and two great-grandchildren.

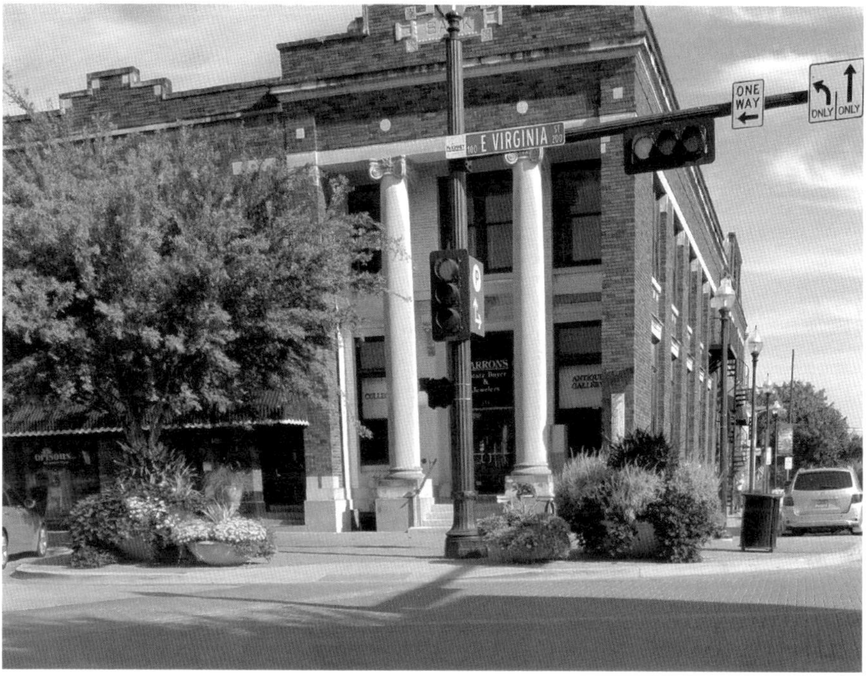


The buildings as they appear today. *Author's collection.*

After many years in the newspaper business, Walter Wilson retired from journalism and worked as McKinney's postmaster, a position he held for four years. When he died at age seventy in 1939, the *Denison Press* wrote this about him:

> *If Heaven needed another worker, then Walter B. Wilson, editor of the* Courier-Gazette, *McKinney, is already at his task. For more than twenty-five years he was known to us and always we have admired him for his quiet, forceful life whose pen moved with the ease that only a well matured mind could prompt, and with the forcefulness of a sage. His manners were as mild as a woman of grace....Such men as Walter B. Wilson come rare in this day and age and the whole state will be the poorer because of his going.*[142]

Sophia Presley stayed in McKinney for many years, supporting herself and her daughter by working as a dressmaker. As late as 1930, she was still living in McKinney, looking after her seventy-five-year-old widowed mother, Mattie, as well as Emma Lou. One of Sophia's sisters, Lula, had moved to Gatesville and married a widower and prominent business owner named Morton Scott. Morton Scott was best known for his furniture store located on Gatesville's town square. The business, much like the Crouch-Hartzog furniture store in McKinney, had added mortuary services to its list of services during the early years, later establishing the derivative as a separate business. Emma's move from McKinney to Gatesville, made sometime during the early 1930s, was likely made in response to her Aunt Lula's beckoning.

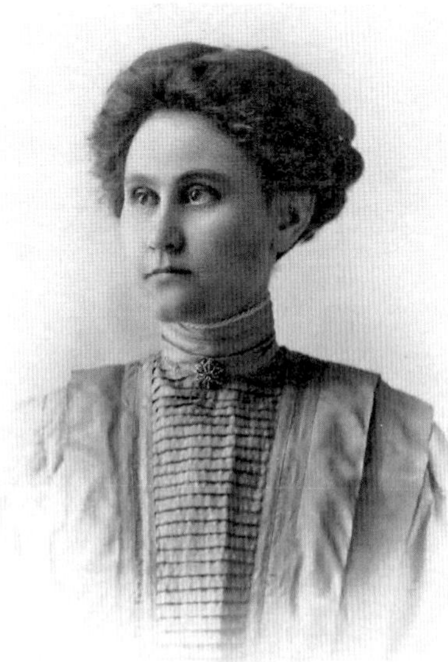

Lula Moore Scott. *Courtesy of Robert M. Scott.*

If Lula was testing her matchmaking skills when she summoned Emma Lou to Gatesville, she must have been pleased with the outcome. In 1937, Emma married Robert Wilkes Scott, Lula's stepson. Robert W. Scott and his sister Lois worked at the family businesses with their father, eventually taking charge of both concerns. The businesses were fixtures in early Gatesville, and the funeral home, though now under ownership outside of the Scott family, still bears the Scott name.

In 1946, when she was sixty-nine, Sophia moved to Gatesville from Dallas, where she had been living for two years. She lived with Emma Lou and Robert, who added two children to the household, Robert and Jane. Sophia died in 1965 at the age of eighty-nine, ending a widowhood of fifty-two years. Emma Lou returned her mother's remains to McKinney for burial, a loving gesture that placed her near Norman after a decades-long separation. Emma Lou outlived her husband and, in 1982, when she was seventy-one years old, married James Murrah, age seventy-eight. She died in 2000.

Emma Lou's son, Robert Morton Scott, an Austinite, was generous in sharing memories about his mother and grandmother for this publication. Although he knew little about the incident that led to the horrific death of his grandfather Robert Norman Presley, his input was valuable. Robert helped sort out pieces of the Scott family history that were rather confusing, and he spent much time unearthing the Presley pictures presented here. Because Emma Lou married her aunt's stepson, Robert's grandmothers were sisters.

He remembered Lula as a severe and demanding woman who did not allow anyone to call her grandmother but recalled Sophia as warm. She taught him to be tough, he said, by never letting him win at checkers or Monopoly, even when the sum of twenty-five cents was at stake. It was a lesson she dispensed many times, probably with a wink, always proclaiming that it was a character-building exercise.

Robert M. Scott also offered two rather unusual facts about his mother, Emma Lou, and his grandmother Sophia. Sophia developed a rather severe hunched back during her life, and Emma Lou was almost entirely deaf. These specifics, while not terribly important, are often the kinds of details that are lost in family history. Emma Lou's hearing problem is significant, because before it was diagnosed, Robert Scott believes it may have been misinterpreted as a cognitive problem. It was another concern heaped on Sophia.

Norman Presley's mother, Emma Jane, died in 1925 at age seventy-eight. After his wife's death, Robert Fulton Presley moved to Dallas to live with two of his daughters, Anna and Crauf, both public school teachers who never married. When he died in 1945 at the age of ninety-eight, Presley was said to have been the last surviving member of a longstanding Dallas Chapter of Confederate Veterans.

Robert and Lelia Hight, the parents of four-year-old victim Russell, lived most of their lives in McKinney; they moved to Dallas about 1930 but soon returned to McKinney. They raised their son Eugene and a daughter named Mary Kathryn. Eugene's daughter Martha Prince and Mary Kathryn's daughter Barbara Ware furnished pictures for this book. Lelia and Robert Hight both died in 1963. Stella Russell, who was Lelia's sister and also a victim of the collapse, remained unmarried throughout her life, living with her parents and one of her grandmothers in Farmersville. Her father, Elijah, was in the real estate business, but he once owned a livery stable in Farmersville and was a member of the local order of the Odd Fellows in Farmersville. Russell held no animosity toward his lodge brothers in McKinney for the death of his grandson and the injury to his daughter. Stella worked as a saleslady for many years and died in 1963 at the age of seventy. She carried the terrible memory of Russell's death with her throughout her life.

Annie Curts married a well-known McKinney resident named Benjamin F. Cloyd, who was ten years her senior, on March 19, 1918. Ben and his brother Joe ran a business their father had started in McKinney in 1870. They sold and repaired farm equipment and, for a short time, sold cars.

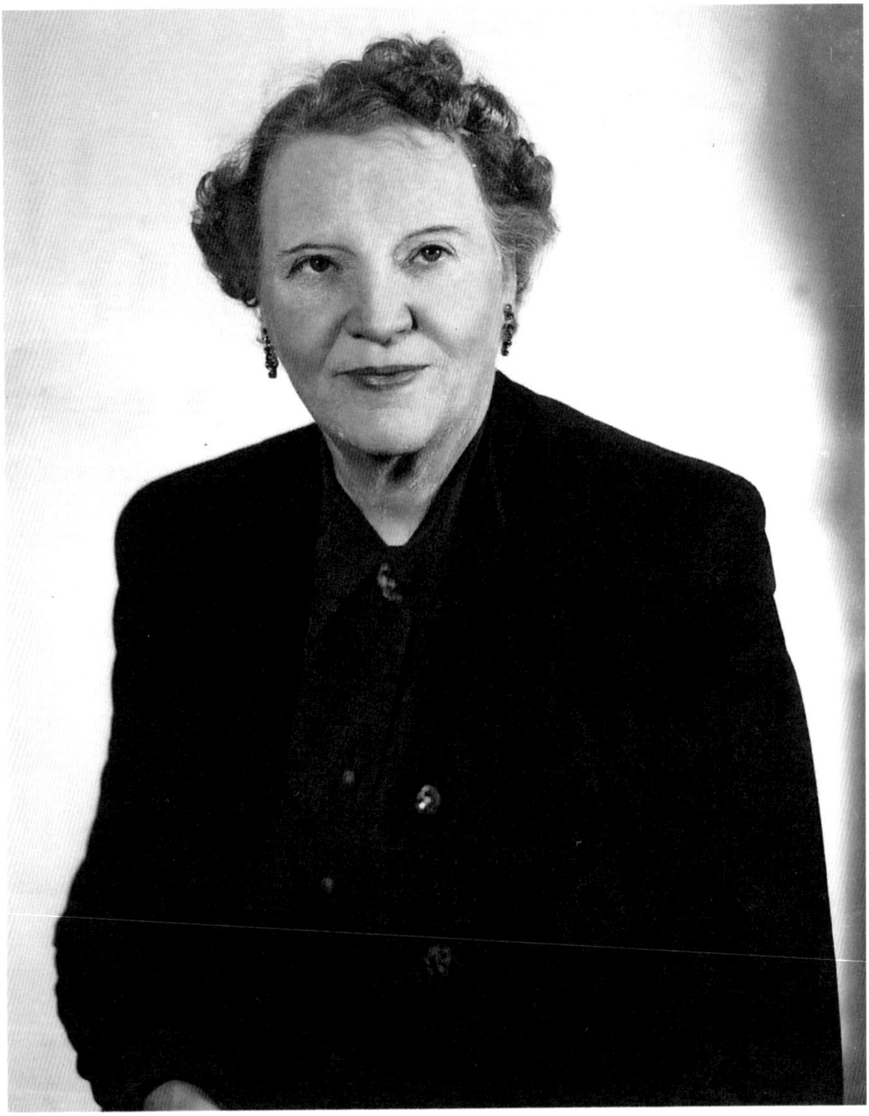

Estelle "Stella" Russell in later years. *Courtesy of Martha Prince.*

Annie's parents moved to Ellis County, and about 1933, she and Ben moved to Dallas. Annie was widowed in 1941. She worked for the Titche-Goettinger Department Store in Dallas, a well-known early chain that later merged with Joske's. She had no children. At the time of her death at age ninety-eight, Annie had been widowed for forty-five years.

Vernie Graves opened his own dry goods store on January 1, 1916. The store, L.V. Graves and Company, was located beneath the phone company in a building across the street from the empty lot where the Odd Fellows building had once stood. Ben Estes joined his longtime friend as an employee—or perhaps an unnamed partner. The store lasted well into the 1920s; unfortunately, Ben Estes did not. He died on October 31, 1920. Six pallbearers and fourteen honorary pallbearers served in his honor, among them Ike Talkington, former mayor Henry Finch, Vernie Graves and John Thomas. Lewis Vernon Graves died on January 16, 1940, at the age of sixty-seven from coronary thrombosis.

John and Stella Thomas, the parents of two sons, lived out their lives in McKinney. Their elder son, Clifford, eventually moved to Fort Worth, but younger son Russell lived most of his life in McKinney, with the exception of a period of time when he lived in Denton. Russell's son, John Mack Thomas of Arlington, was instrumental in locating several pictures for this publication and shared some of his memories of McKinney and of his grandfather. John Mack was born in a hospital across the street from his grandparents' home, and he remembered spending many hours on their front porch on Parker Street. His father, Russell, had often played at the old Kirkpatrick home and oversized barn at the end of the street. In May 1913, just three months after his father's close brush with death, fourteen-year-old Russell carved his name into a rung of a wooden ladder in the barn. Many years later, the owner of the property, a third-generation Kirkpatrick, gave the rung to John Mack Thomas, who still proudly displays the keepsake on the wall of his deck. John Mack said that his grandfather talked about the early days in McKinney but rarely mentioned the event in 1913. It was, no doubt, an unpleasant memory he did not wish to resurrect.

John Waller Thomas, the only male to survive being trapped within the rubble, died in 1953 at the age of eighty-eight from arteriosclerosis. He is buried beside his beloved Stella, who lived to be ninety-nine, in the Pecan Grove Cemetery in McKinney.

Belle McWilliams lived to be ninety-eight. She remained in McKinney, where she died in 1959 from circulatory failure. Belle's son John McWilliams became an army chaplain. John's two sons, both graduates of West Point, also served the U.S. Army with distinction, one reaching the rank of brigadier general.

Luther Stephenson joined the army and worked as a harness and saddle maker at Camp Travis during a portion of World War I. He was adept at working with his hands, particularly with leather, working for a time at a shoe repair shop. He married Flossie Rains in 1918, and the couple had three children: Marcella, George and Mary "Bess." Bess Miller, who lives in Denton, is unique as the only second-generation survivor of the victims of the collapse. She was most helpful in locating some wonderful pictures of her father. Bess knew only scant details about the collapsed building from which her father escaped.

At some point, the Stephenson family changed the spelling of their name to Stevenson. Later in his life, Luther became skilled at painting cars and opened his own auto-painting garage in Denton. He died in 1980.

Lula Searcy never married. Her father died the year following the tragedy, and she continued to live with her mother and siblings until her mother's death in 1936. Lula also worked as a cashier and bookkeeper in dry goods stores for many years, living with one of her sisters and their brother Leonard. She died at the age of seventy-five in 1956, the victim of colon cancer, and is buried in Pecan Grove Cemetery.

Lula Bush, the widow of Leslie Walker Bush, lived until 1936. During her last years, Lula lived in McKinney with her youngest child, a daughter named Leslie, who was married to Mac Moran Hill, a grain dealer. The couple had one son in 1924, the namesake of his father.

Fannie Graves, mother of victim Iva Kistler and grandmother to Annie Kistler, died in 1927. Iva died in 1936 at the age of fifty-four from complications of high blood pressure. Annie Kistler, who was four when she was caught in the collapse, became a teacher, married Earl Cameron Helms in 1934 and moved to nearby Celina. Earl Helms owned a funeral home for many years. He and Annie had two children: a daughter, Iva Ann, born in 1936, and a son, Cameron, born in 1941. Tragically, Cameron was killed in a car accident in 1958 when he was just seventeen. Iva Ann Helms Bell had no children, ending this line of Kistler descendants.

Cassie Seay became a member of a large and prominent local family when she wed William Avery Dowell sometime before 1930. Avery was one of four sons of J.P. Dowell, the owner of a hardware store that was established in 1873 and grew into one of the leading businesses in McKinney. The couple had no children. Cassie died in 1950.

Although the injuries Iva Shirley received in the collapse were quite serious, she recovered after a few weeks, but her husband, Mort, was not so fortunate, as he never fully recovered from the injuries he had sustained in a train wreck in 1899. He became ill in 1920 and died at the age of fifty-two. The couple's son, Jack, who at age five had barely missed being a victim in the collapse, became a naval officer. Jack had two sons: Jack Jr. and Robert.

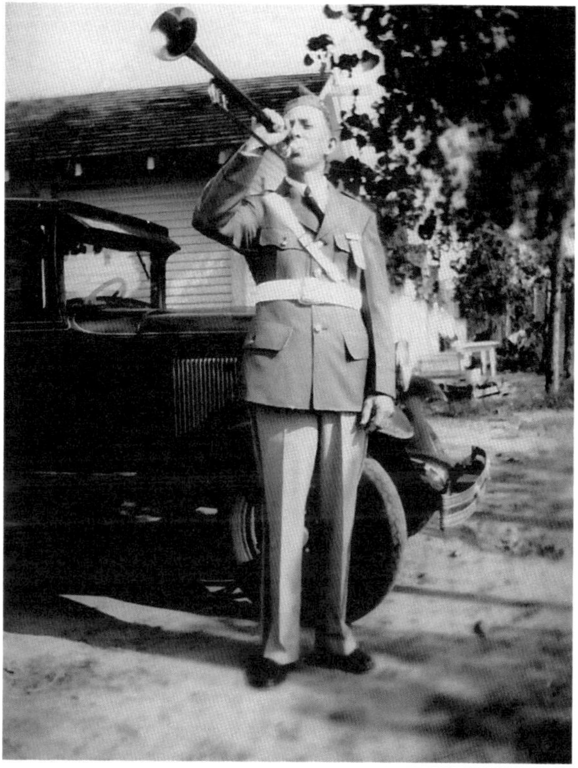

*Right*: Luther Stephenson in later years as a member of the American Legion. *Courtesy of Bess Miller.*

*Below*: Luther Stephenson working in a shoe shop. *Courtesy of Bess Miller.*

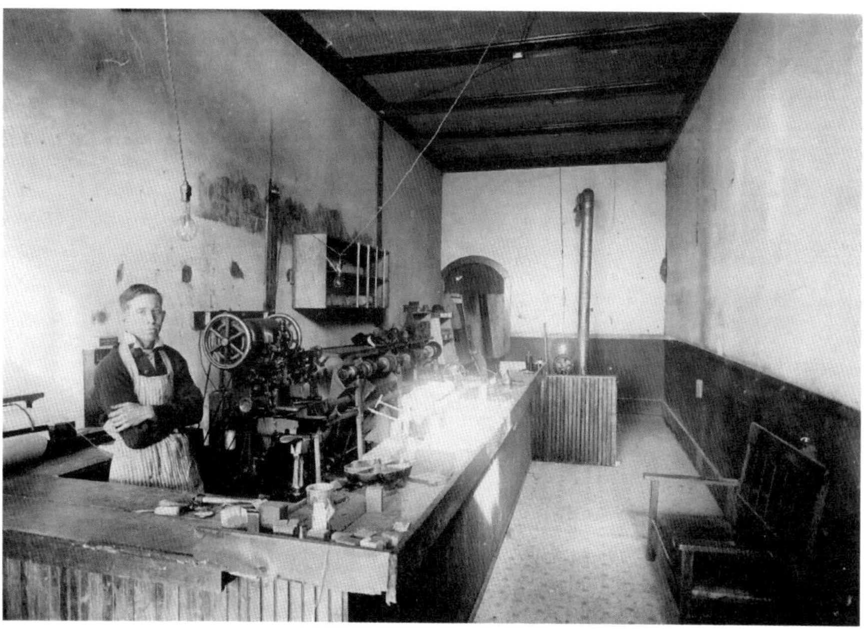

Robert Shirley lives in Tyler, Texas, and supplied the information about his grandfather's unfortunate life-changing injuries from a train derailment. Jack Junior's wife, Nan, also furnished information.

Iva lived to be ninety, eventually moving into the home of her daughter Gladys in McKinney. Iva Shirley outlived her husband by forty-four years and is buried beside him in McKinney's Pecan Grover Cemetery.

Jennie Barnett raised her two children, Lillian and Fayett, and never remarried. She apparently supported herself and children by farming. When the children were grown, she moved to Plano to live with her son and later to Greenville to live with her daughter. She died in 1958. Further information regarding Lyda Moreland, Jennie's shopping companion that day, eluded this writer.

The mystery of the identity of Lyda Moreland is not the only one associated with this story. In chapter 7, John Thompson's amazing story of survival included an unidentified woman customer. In an interview he gave the local newspaper soon after the collapse, Thomas outlined his ordeal, naming the victims he had encountered while trapped in the rubble. The exception was the female customer who had been pushed into the front showcase, whose name he did not know.

Who was that unnamed customer who communicated with and was later rescued alongside John Thomas and Annie Curts? An analysis using the process of elimination may solve this riddle. A complete list of women customers who were in the building when it fell includes Kate Milligan, Rosa Welch, Bessie Wade, Ira Kistler, Fannie Graves, Cassie Seay, Lyda Moreland, Jennie Barnett and Iva Shirley. The mystery lady was not badly injured and was mobile, moving to the center of the store and back to the front with Thomas and Curts. This eliminates those who were killed outright and those who were pinned so badly that they required rescue workers to free them. Female customers in that category were Kate Milligan, Rosa Welch and Bessie Wade.

As Thomas, Curts and their female companion made their way back to the front of the store to escape the heat, the fire became large enough to illuminate the space near the front doors. For the first time, Thomas and the others could actually see other victims. Thomas specifically stated that he had seen three additional women at that time. He recognized Cassie Seay and called out to her and believed the others were Eva Searcy and Iva Shirley. Therefore, we can also eliminate these three because Thomas clearly knew their names. Lyda Moreland and Jennie Barnett, the last of the ten female customers listed above, were located near the back of the store and exited the building from the east side with slight assistance from rescuers. Iva Kistler was trapped with her four-year-old daughter, Annie, so she, too, can be eliminated.

The mystery customer had to have been Fannie Graves. Fannie had come into the store with her daughter Iva Kistler and four-year-old granddaughter, Annie. The three were in the front of the store when the building fell. John Thomas and Iva Shirley both said that they had heard little Annie Kistler talking with her mother, but neither made mention of the grandmother. Fannie must have been pushed into the showcase window in the front of the store.

The jury, after seeing all of the evidence and hearing the testimony of witnesses, concluded that the accident had occurred because the Odd Fellows building was in a dangerous state of ill repair. With that in mind, reexamining the plight of Thomas J. Tingle is a sad exercise. The verdict came too late for him to save his business, avoid legal fees or salvage his reputation in McKinney. He had been publically blamed for irresponsibly storing heavy equipment on the second floor, creating a stigma that a belated apology from newspapers could not erase. He had specifically been accused of causing the shared wall to fail. But the Bates Building had two such walls. After the collapse, the seventeen-inch shared wall on Tingle's west side still stood tall, so much so that it supported large pieces of intact flooring that still bore the weight of several pieces of Tingle's inventory. The wall of the third floor of the Odd Fellows building was only thirteen inches, yet lodge members felt comfortable storing an iron safe on that floor while chastising Tingle for storing inventory on his second floor.

Aside from the jury's verdict, perhaps the best means we have today for reevaluating the reason for the collapse is found in an unlikely place: Walter Wilson's diary. Wilson's assigned no blame to Thomas Tingle or the Bates Building. There are two good reasons to give credence to Wilson's opinion as to the cause of the building's failure. First, Wilson's view was candid because he never expected his private thoughts to be part of the record on this subject, and second, he had information about the condition of the building on good authority. Ike Talkington, the man who supervised much work at the Odd Fellows building, including the installation of the new ceiling just a week before the collapse, was Walter Wilson's brother-in-law. Talkington spent the night at Wilson's home on the night following the accident, and the collapse surely was a topic of discussion. Under other circumstances, Wilson's view might be seen as no more valuable

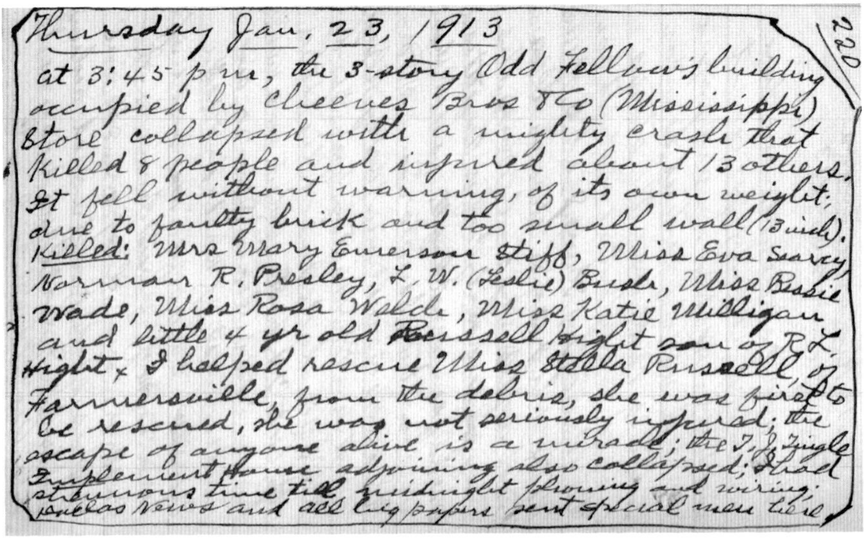
Thursday Jan. 23, 1913 220
at 3:45 p m, the 3-story Odd Fellow's building occupied by Cheeves Bros & Co (Mississippi) Store collapsed with a mighty crash that killed 8 people and injured about 13 others. It fell without warning, of its own weight; due to faulty brick and too small wall (13 inch). Killed: Mrs Mary Emerson Stiff, Miss Eva Searcy, Norman R. Presley, L. W. (Leslie) Bush, Miss Bessie Wade, Miss Rosa Welch, Miss Katie Milligan and little 4 yr old Russell Hight son of R. L. Hight. I helped rescue Miss Stella Russell, of Farmersville, from the debris, she was first to be rescued, she was not seriously injured; the escape of anyone alive is a miracle; the T. J. Zingle Implement House adjoining also collapsed; I had strenuous time till midnight phoning and wiring; Dallas News and all big papers sent special men here.

Walter Wilson recorded these words in his diary on the night of the accident. *Walter B. Wilson Collection, Briscoe Center for American History, University of Texas at Austin.*

than anyone else's. But the specifics he wrote in his journal were brief and precise, suggesting that he was confident in his assessment.

Much of Walter B. Wilson's work is included in the body of McKinney's recorded history, but perhaps nothing he wrote is more significant than the words he entered into his diary shortly after midnight on January 23, 1913: "It fell without warning, of its own weight; due to faulty brick and too small wall (13 inch)."[143]

# NOTES

## *Preface*

1. *McKinney Democrat-Gazette* 30, no. 51, ed. 1, January 23, 1913, accessed through University of North Texas Libraries, The Portal to Texas History [hereafter UNT]. Walter Wilson was an advocate for schools in McKinney, serving on the school board for over thirty years.

## *Chapter 1*

2. *Dallas Weekly Herald* 22, no. 42, p. 1, July 3, 1875, accessed through GenealogyBank.com [hereafter GB]; *Denison Daily Cresset* 1, no. 295, ed. 1, p. 1, June 28, 1875, UNT.
3. Ibid. This quote, taken from the above referenced *Cresset*, asserts that the courthouse was still under construction in June 1875: "Work on McKinney courthouse is rapidly progressing." A dance held on New Year's 1876 celebrated the building's completion.
4. *Dallas Weekly Herald* 22, p. 2, September 26, 1874, GB.
5. *Dallas Weekly Herald* 27, no. 9, p. 2, November 13, 1869, GB. Note Abraham Rhine's son Benjamin was also a merchant in McKinney for many years.
6. *McKinney Advocate* 4, no. 1, ed. 1, April 3, 1880, UNT.
7. *Galveston Tri-Weekly News* 28, no. 142, p. 1, August 1, 1870, GB.
8. *San Antonio Express* 9, no. 44, October 20, 1875, GB.

9. Hall and Hall, *Collin County*, 112. According to the Halls, the square was commonly called the court square.
10. Ibid., 51.
11. *McKinney Advocate* 4, no. 1, ed. 1, April 3, 1880, UNT. Peter Turbitt was born in Ireland about 1847 according to census records. In June 1878, he traveled to Chicago, where he married Bridget Alice Buckley before returning to McKinney. The Turbitt name is sometimes spelled Turbit and Turbet in various records and news articles.
12. Sophy Presley vs. Cheeves Bros. & Co., ET AL, Forty-Fourth Judicial District Court, Dallas, Dallas Library, History and Archives Division, case #19028, microfilm file box number 420. This lengthy set of court documents resulted from a lawsuit filed as a result of the accident. The text contains some elements of the building's history.

## *Chapter 2*

13. *Dallas Weekly Herald* 21, no. 38, p. 1, June 6, 1874, GB.
14. Ibid. 22, no. 42, p. 1, July 3, 1875, GB.
15. *Dallas Morning News*, 2D, June 17, 1968, GB; *Dallas Daily Herald* 2, no. 52, ed. 1, April 11, 1872, UNT. The *Herald* features an ad for the Dallas Planing (*sic*) Mills, including mention of the contracting/building services of P.H. Jamison. The *News* featured an article about the partnership and the brickmaking business.
16. Presley vs. Cheeves Bros.
17. *The Democrat* 8, no. 16, ed. 1, May 28, 1891, UNT.
18. U.S. City Directories, 1822–1995; Dallas, Texas, City Directory 1889, 467, accessed through Ancestry.com.
19. *Weekly Democrat-Gazette* 30, no. 52, ed. 1, January 30, 1913, UNT.
20. Presley vs. Cheeves Bros.
21. *Sherman Daily Democrat* 36, ed. 1, October 31, 1916, UNT. The assets and liabilities of the local Odd Fellows lodge were listed in this newspaper. At that time, their properties were encumbered by liens totalling $8,500.
22. Murphy and Perry were married to sisters whose maiden name was Freeman.
23. Murphy's son-in-law James was widowed in 1893 when Mattie died at age twenty-three, leaving him with their three-year-old son, Roe. George Murphy and his wife, Mary, raised the child.

24. The data about ownership changes came from various local newspapers for the period.
25. *The Democrat* 13, no. 52, ed. 1, January 28, 1897, UNT.
26. *McKinney Democrat-Gazette* 10, no. 45, ed. 1, December 25, 1897, UNT.
27. *The Democrat* 20, no. 1, ed. 1, February 5, 1903, UNT. Ben Estes seems to have had a connection to the Mississippi Store that went beyond that of simple employee. It is not a significant point but an interesting one. In this case, the lease that ran from 1904 until 1912 was in the names of William Purnell, Ben Estes and Vernie Graves.
28. Ibid.

## *Chapter 3*

29. Ibid. 7, no. 9, ed. 1, April 3, 1890, UNT. Other saloons listed were Standard Gauge, Elm, Rambo, A.L. Cole, Uncle Burl, Parlor and Howard and Williams; Barnhart and Estes, *McKinney*, 8. In earlier days, when the town was temporarily populated with railroad workers, there were twenty or more saloons on the town square.
30. *McKinney Advocate* 4, no. 1, ed. 1, April 3, 1880, UNT.
31. Peter Turbitt may have fallen on hard times. He sold his saloon building in 1885 and put his farm and another commercial property up for sale the following year. He remained in McKinney and in the saloon business until at least 1890. Sometime after 1890, he and Alice moved to Wisconsin and later Chicago. By 1903, Alice was widowed.
32. Pictures of C.D. Bates, Lea and the couple's three children (when adults) are posted on this website: https://www.geni.com/people/Constantine-Dixon-Bates-Jr/4822457458000043000. The descendant who posted these pictures is deceased, and I could locate no other family members
33. Deed Records, Collin County Clerks Office, book 196, page 324.
34. Ibid., book 28, page 27.
35. Sanborn maps for McKinney, 1892, sheet 4, accessed on June 5, 2017, at this website: http://www.lib.utexas.edu/maps/sanborn/texas.html
36. *The Democrat* 5, no. 21, ed. 1, June 21, 1888, UNT. The newspaper characterized Bates as a prominent man in the cotton business and an esteemed citizen.
37. Texas Wills and Probate Records, 1833–1974, accessed through Ancestry.com.
38. *Weekly Democrat-Gazette* 25, no. 13, ed. 1, April 30, 1908, UNT.
39. Deed Records, Collin County Clerks Office, book 196, page 325.

40. The terms of Mr. Tingle's lease were included in court documents pertaining to a lawsuit.

## *Chapter 4*

41. *The Democrat* 23, no. 11, ed. 1, April 12, 1906, UNT. This newspaper features an article about the Cheeves store, listing the names of the store's ten employees in 1906.
42. Ibid. 13, no. 50, ed. 1, January 14, 1897, UNT.
43. *Weekly Democrat-Gazette* 37, ed. 1, December 4, 1920, UNT. The information in this paragraph was taken from Ben's 1920 obituary.
44. *The Democrat* 13, no. 50, ed. 1, January 14, 1897, UNT. A list of creditors in the bankruptcy of Perry, Oldham and Company, includes employees who were owed wages. The list includes four employees who were still employed at the store in 1913: Ben Estes, John Thomas, Belle McWilliams and Vernie Graves. Assuming continuous employment, these four had each worked for the Mississippi a minimum of sixteen years in 1913.
45. *Weekly Democrat-Gazette* 30, no. 49, ed. 1, January 9, 1913, UNT.
46. *The Democrat* 16, no. 42, ed. 1, November 16, 1899, UNT.
47. *Weekly Democrat-Gazette* 24, no. 6, ed. 1, March 14, 1907, UNT.
48. Ibid. 30, no. 52, ed. 1, January 30, 1913, UNT. This article states that clothing and the millinery department were located on the second level of the store.

## *Chapter 5*

49. *McKinney Democrat-Gazette* 30, no. 51, ed. 1, January 23, 1913, UNT.
50. In 1913, McKinney had five schools, including Central Ward. The others were the high school, two new schools known as the north and south ward schools and a separate school for black children.
51. *McKinney Democrat-Gazette*, "Time Propitious for a New School," 30, no. 51, ed. 1, January 23, 1913, UNT.
52. McKinney Ice Co. vs. Montgomery, https://casetext.com/case/mckinney-ice-light-coal-v-montgomery
53. Hall and Hall, *Collin County*, 220–21.
54. John McKinney, both father and son, were known around town as Uncle John and Uncle Johnny. The "uncle" moniker was rather common in

McKinney at that time. This information gleaned from browsing hundred of McKinney newspaper articles.

55. Vargo, *McKinney, Texas*, 27–28.

56. *Weekly Democrat-Gazette* 31, no. 48, ed. 1, January 7, 1915, UNT. This article makes reference to firemen sleeping in the courthouse.

57. Ibid., 30, no. 52, ed. 1, January 30, 1913, UNT.

## *Chapter 6*

58. *McKinney Examiner* 27, no. 10, ed. 1, January 30, 1913, UNT. Annie's memory of looking at the clock just seconds before the collapse helped establish the exact time of the accident.

59. Ibid. Annie's words were, "Somehow, perhaps it was intuition, I was moved to look toward the north walls, right at the front, and I saw it begin to move inward." The Cheeves store faced south, so the north wall would have actually been the back wall of the store. Annie clarified by saying she was referring to the "front walls" of the store. It is interesting that she spoke of the front wall in plural, perhaps because the showcase windows on the ground level of the building took up much of the front façade, making it seem like there were walls on either side of those display windows.

60. *Weekly Democrat-Gazette* 30, no. 52, ed. 1, January 30, 1913, UNT. Mr. Bomar later owned one of the first gas stations in McKinney.

61. Ibid.

62. *Dallas Morning News* 28, no. 116, p. 1, January 24, 1913, GB.

63. *Weekly Democrat-Gazette* 30, no. 52, ed. 1, January 30, 1913, UNT.

64. Joy Gough, "Disaster in McKinney, Collapse of the Odd Fellows Hall," Texas State Genealogical Society *Stirpes* 37, no. 4 (December 1997): 5. This account states that Graves literally ran directly to the newspaper office after he emerged from the wreckage. The *Cleveland Leader*, *Fort Worth Star Telegram* and *Norwich Bulletin* quoted Graves, the *Leader* offering this: "Vernie Graves, said to be the only occupant of the store when the crash came who escaped unhurt, stated positively that fifty persons were in the place when the walls fell." *Fort Worth Star Telegram* 31, no. 10, p. 4, January 24, 1913, GB.

65. *McKinney Examiner* 27, no. 10, ed. 2, January 30, 1913, UNT.

66. Ibid., ed. 1, January 30, 1913, UNT.

## Chapter 7

67. Ibid., ed. 2, January 30, 1913, UNT. Note: The *Examiner* conducted a lengthy interview with John Thomas and published it in this special edition. It is the most comprehensive version of his story.
68. Ibid. Annie later stated that she was surprised at her own calm.
69. Ibid.
70. The identity of this customer will be discussed in a later chapter.
71. Ibid.
72. *Weekly Democrat-Gazette* 30, no. 52, ed. 1, January 30, 1913, UNT.
73. *McKinney Examiner* 27, no. 10, ed. 2, January 30, 1913, UNT.
74. Gough, "Disaster in McKinney," 5.

## Chapter 8

75. Mary was also listed as Marie in some records. Her tombstone identifies her as Mary. She may have been called Marie to distinguish her from her mother, who was also named Mary. The Crouch-Hartzog undertaking establishment was owned by Isaac Crouch and F.H. Hartzog. Also, the two men were partners in a hardware/furniture store that was located on the south side of the town square. It was not unusual for hardware store owners to provide mortuary services in the early days, a service that was a natural offshoot because they sold caskets.
76. *McKinney Examiner* 27, no. 10, ed.1, January 30, 1913, UNT.
77. Death certificates accessed through Ancestry.com. Dr. Hunter, who had lived for six years in nearby Malissa, moved to McKinney in February 1906. In 1913, Dr. Hunter was practicing in partnership with Dr. W.S. Wysong in an office located on the Morrow block in downtown McKinney.
78. *McKinney Examiner* 27, no. 10, ed. 1, January 30, 1913, UNT.
79. There is a curious narrative about Rosa Welch attached to her burial site information on the internet. It states that she was the "sole dependence of her father and brothers to hold the home" because her mother had died just a few months prior. According to records, including her mother's obituary, Bessie died in 1908, almost five years before the accident that killed Rosa.
80. *Weekly Democrat-Gazette* 30, no. 52, ed. 1, January 30, 1913, UNT. The caption below a picture of Miss Wade states that she was "soon to be married."

81. *McKinney Examiner* 27, no. 10, ed. 1, January 30, 1913, UNT.
82. Bush's probate records were located on Ancestry.com.
83. Horn journal. Copies of the pages of the journal used for this text were supplied by two of Horn's great-grandchildren, Amoret Cain and Clyde Geer.
84. *McKinney Examiner* 27, no. 10, ed. 1, January 30, 1913, UNT.

## *Chapter 9*

85. *Bartlett Tribune and News*, March 19, 1926. Many Temple residents remember the location of the restaurant as the former domicile of the Temple Cheeves store, which it was for many years. However, before the Cheeves enterprise moved to this space, it was housed in one of the largest buildings in Temple, located at Second Street and Avenue A. The three-story brick, owned by Patrick and Thomas Cheeves, covered an entire block. At its peak, the store carried, groceries, tinware, glassware and furniture in addition to the standard inventory of clothing and accessories. When the brothers sold the building to Frank Doering in March 1926, they had been operating their store in the large building, which later came to be known as the Doering Building, for over twenty-five years.
86. Cheeves Bros. Steak House, located in space once occupied by a Cheeves Brothers store, is known for its first-class food and service. The Cheeves brothers were not in the restaurant business (although they did later add groceries to their line of goods at some locations), but there is little doubt that they would approve of the association between this upscale eatery and their name.
87. *Texas Genealogical Records*, Ellis County, vol. 21, 1680–1968, p. 200.
88. *Southwestern Reporter* 25, 1894, West Publishing Company, St. Paul, 325–26.
89. *Temple Times* 17, no. 1, ed. 1, December 3, 1897, UNT. This newspaper contained an ad for the Temple store, listing "branch houses" in Mexia and Cameron as well as Cheeves and Linthicum stores in Marlin, Calver and Taylor. The Waxahachie store operated under the name Cheeves and Cluck.
90. *Temple Times* 12, no. 40, ed. 1, UNT. An ad for Cheeves Bros. announcing "April 1, we will open a complete line of dry goods."
91. *Dallas Morning News*, March 27, 1893, 3. Mr. Wilkerson purchased the building from W.A. Masters of Galveston on March 25, 1893, at a cost of $2,500.
92. *Weekly Democrat-Gazette* 20, no. 1, ed. 1, February 5, 1903, UNT.

## *Chapter 10*

93. *Dallas Morning News* 28, no. 117, January 25, 1913, GB.
94. Ibid.
95. Walter Wilson's diary, Walter B. Wilson Collection, di_11036, Dolph Briscoe Center for American History, University of Texas at Austin.
96. *Temple Daily Telegram* 6, no. 58, ed. 1, January 24, 1913, UNT.
97. *McKinney Examiner* 27, no. 10, ed. 1, January 30, 1913, UNT.
98. Ibid.
99. *Weekly Democrat-Gazette* 30, no. 2, ed. 1, February 13, 1913, UNT.
100. The news that was reprinted was a week old and contained several errors. It must have been confusing to people reading it and confronting the newer information that in some cases contradicted portions of the older data. The *Examiner* disclosed its source in small print that may not have been obvious to readers.
101. *Fort Worth Star Telegram* 31, no. 10, p. 4, January 24, 1913, GB.
102. Ibid.
103. *McKinney Examiner* 27, no. 10, ed. 1, January 30, 1913, UNT.
104. *Cleveland Leader* 67, no. 24, January 24, 1913, GB.
105. *Elkhart (IN) Daily Review*, January 25, 1913, 3, GB.
106. *Times-Picayune* (New Orleans, LA) 76, no. 366, January 24, 1913, GB.
107. *McKinney Examiner* 27, no. 10, ed. 1, January 30, 1913, UNT.
108. Walter Wilson's diary.
109. *McKinney Examiner* 27, no. 10, ed. 1, January 30, 1913, UNT.
110. Ibid.

## *Chapter 11*

111. A copy of Tingle's agreement with Avery & Sons was included with other documents related to a 1916 trial. Tingle had $4,000 worth of insurance, but it may not have covered damage due to a collapsed building.
112. *Automotive Manufacturer* 55 (May 1913): 75.
113. *McKinney Examiner* 27, no. 10, ed. 1, January 30, 1913, UNT.
114. *Fort Worth Star-Telegram* 31, no. 10, p. 4, January 24, 1913, GB.
115. *Weekly Democrat-Gazette* 30, no. 52, ed. 1, January 30, 1913, UNT.
116. *McKinney Examiner* 27, no. 10, ed. 2, January 30, 1913, UNT. The local papers published these and other remarks as they appeared in other newspapers.

117. Ibid.
118. *McKinney Examiner* 27, no. 10, ed. 1, January 30, 1913, UNT.
119. *McKinney Democrat-Gazette* 30, no. 2, ed. 1, February 13, 1913, UNT.
120. *Dallas Morning News* 29, no. 2, October 2, 1913, GB.
121. *Weekly Democrat-Gazette* 31, no. 21, ed. 1, June 25, 1914, UNT.

## *Chapter 12*

122. Presley vs. Cheeves Bros. Note: There are several things contained in this microfilm file, comprising over two hundred pages. It contains a mixture of documents including the charges leveled by the Presleys and the response to those charges by the lodge. Other papers include the questions posed to people who were deposed and the questions asked them at trial. Some specific questions posed to the jury were also included with this file. Most of the information in this chapter was obtained from this source.
123. Answers offered by the lodge to the charges made in Presley vs. Cheeves Bros.
124. Ibid.
125. Ibid.
126. Ibid.
127. Ibid.
128. Ibid.
129. Ibid.
130. Ibid.
131. *McKinney Examiner* 27, no. 10, ed. 1, January 30, 1913, UNT.
132. Presley vs. Cheeves Bros.
133. Ibid.
134. *Weekly Democrat-Gazette* 33, ed. 1, October 12, 1916, UNT. Note: Although the records I located on this case numbered well over two hundred pages, there was no transcript of the actual testimony included in the file. Therefore, I relied on the information in the depositions, attorneys' questions made from the depositions and other documents for information given by witnesses at trial.

## *Chapter 13*

135. *Weekly Democrat-Gazette* 34, ed. 1, August 30, 1917, UNT.

136. *Sherman Daily Democrat* 36, ed. 1, November 3, 1916, UNT.
137. Presley vs. Cheeves Bros.
138. *Weekly Democrat-Gazette* 33, ed. 1, December 28, 1916, UNT.
139. Ibid., November 30, 1916, UNT.
140. Ibid., December 28, 1916, UNT.

## *Chapter 14*

141. Ibid. 36, ed. 1, January, 22, 1920, UNT.
142. *Denison Press* 6, no. 101, ed. 1, October 21, 1939, UNT.
143. Walter Wilson's diary.

# BIBLIOGRAPHY


## *Books*

Barnhart, Ryan, and Ryan Estes, *McKinney*. Charleston, SC: Arcadia Publishing, 2010.

Bush, Nancy, and Joyce Bush Benton Morian. *The Bush Family: Ancestors & Descendants of Leslie Walker Bush*. Self-published, 1989.

Hall, Helen Gibbard, and the Collin County Historical Society Inc. *The Way It All Began, McKinney, Texas: A History*. McKinney, TX: Collin County Historical Society, 2010.

Hall, Roy F., and Helen Gibbard Hall. *Collin County: Pioneering in North Texas*. Quanah, TX: Nortex Press, 1975.

Vargo, Julia L. *McKinney, Texas, The First 150 Years*. Virginia Beach, VA: Donning Company Publishers, 1997.

## *Newspapers*

*Bartlett Tribune and News*

*Cleveland Leader*

*Dallas Daily Herald*

*Dallas Morning News*

*Dallas Weekly Herald*

*The Democrat* (McKinney, TX)

*Denison Daily Cresset*
*Denison Press*
*Elkhart (IN) Daily Review*
*Fort Worth Star-Telegram*
*Galveston Tri-Weekly News*
*McKinney Advocate*
*McKinney Examiner*
*Norwich (CT) Bulletin*
*San Antonio Express*
*Sherman Daily Democrat*
*Temple Daily Telegram*
*Temple Times*
*Times-Picayune* (New Orleans, LA)
*Weekly Democrat-Gazette*

## *Magazines, Journals and other Periodicals*

*Automotive Manufacturer*, 1913
*Collin Chronicles*, 1996–97
*Dallas, Texas City Directory*, 1889
*Southwestern Reporter*, 1894
*Texas Genealogical Records, Ellis County*

## *Articles*

Gough, Joy. "Disaster in McKinney, Collapse of the Odd Fellows Hall." Texas State Genealogical Society, *Stirpes* 37, no. 4 (December 1997): 3–10.

## *Other*

Sanborn Maps

## *Interviews*

JOY GOUGH, local historian in McKinney
ED HINKLE, widower of Patsy Cheeves Hinkle
BESS MILLER, daughter of Luther Stephenson
DAVID MILLER, distant relative to Ike Talkington
MARTHA PRINCE, daughter of Eugene Hight, cousin to Russell Hight, great-niece to Stella Russell
FEROL HINKLE RICHARDSON, great-granddaughter of Patrick Cheeves
ROBERT MORTON SCOTT, grandson of Robert Norman and Sophia Presley
ROBERT SHIRLEY, son of Jack Shirley, grandson of Mort and Iva Shirley
JOHN MACK THOMAS, grandson of John Waller Thomas
BARBARA WARE, daughter of Mary Kathryn Hight, cousin to Russell Hight, great-niece to Stella Russell

# INDEX

## A



## B



## C

## K



## L



## M



## N



## O



## P



## R

# ABOUT THE AUTHOR

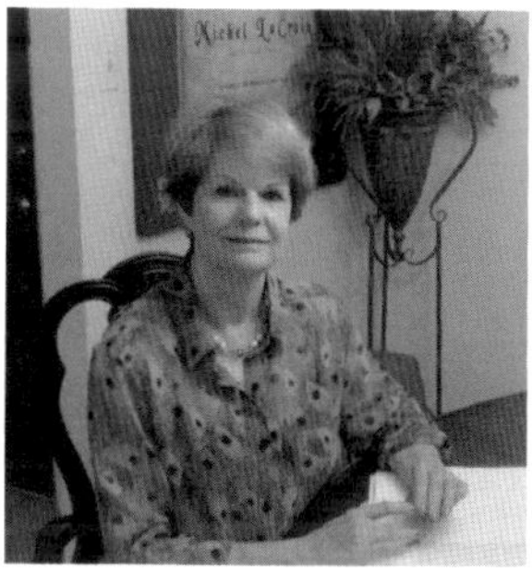

Carol Wilson is an enthusiast of Texas history with two previous books to her credit: *In the Governor's Shadow: The True History of Ma and Pa Ferguson* and *The Stage Stops Here: The History of the Stagecoach Inn, Salado, TX.* Carol is a graduate of Mary Hardin-Baylor, a Texas CPA, retired, and a former certified fraud examiner. She lives in Temple with her husband, Guy, but spends much time in Florida, where the couple's two grown daughters reside.

*Visit us at*
www.historypress.com